WHITE OR RED:
ITS ALL IN YOUR HEAD

WHITE OR RED: ITS ALL IN YOUR HEAD

A Crisp and Refreshing Book about Wine

CHRIS MILLIKEN

WHITE OR RED: IT'S ALL IN YOUR HEAD
A CRISP AND REFRESHING BOOK ABOUT WINE

iUniverse books may be ordered through booksellers or by contacting:

iUniverse
1663 Liberty Drive
Bloomington, IN 47403
www.iuniverse.com
1-800-Authors (1-800-288-4677)

ISBN: 978-1-4917-9915-4 (sc)
ISBN: 978-1-4917-9916-1 (e)

Library of Congress Control Number: 2016910156

Print information available on the last page.

iUniverse rev. date: 08/04/2016

To my wonderful family and fantastic friends all over the world: thank you for your guidance throughout my life and your patience and support as I wrote this book.

I am truly grateful—cheers to you!

CONTENTS

Introduction ix

How I Became a Wine Producer xi

Part I: About Wine

Chapter 1: A Brief History of Wine.................................... 3
Chapter 2: The Great Grape.. 8
Chapter 3: From Vine to Wine: The Wine-Making Process.............. 15
Chapter 4: Don't Judge a Wine by Its Label........................ 29

Part II: Buying Wine

Chapter 1: So You Know What You Like: Isn't That Enough? 41
Chapter 2: Where to Buy Wine.. 46
Chapter 3: Wine Pairing from a Chef's Point of View 54

Part III: Drinking Wine

Chapter 1: The Wine Survival Kit....................................... 61
Chapter 2: At Your Service 68
Chapter 3: What's in Your Glass? How to Evaluate Wine like a Pro..... 75
Chapter 4: Wine and Dine: How to Order Wine in Restaurants 82

Conclusion.. 91

Bonus Content.. 93
    More Wine Grape Varieties 93
    Wine-Tasting Terminology... 96
    First-Time Wine Drinker's List....................................... 98
    Food-and-Wine Pairings... 99

Index 105

INTRODUCTION

Wine is an amazing and complex journey that twists and turns, starts and stops, and changes daily in so many ways. I have been in the wine industry for many years. I have heard so much, seen so much, tasted so much—and the vine keeps growing. No one knows everything about wine; even those with advanced degrees in wine have much more to learn. On the other hand, wine is just simple fermented grape juice. It's nothing to be afraid of. Whether you're a grape farmer, a winemaker, a cork supplier, a sommelier, a waiter or bartender, a restaurant owner, a hotel manager, a wine shop owner, a collector, or just an occasional wine drinker, every experience is unique.

This book is the result of conversations about food and wine with thousands of people around the world, a product of formal discussions and long, casual dinner parties. Wine is social and therefore conversational; I recall so many evenings that turned into early-morning discussions about wine. After so many exchanges with so many people, I started to notice some patterns. There are many erroneous perceptions about wine. Clever marketing, aficionado perspectives, and opulent desires have created a shrouded industry like no other. I hope to clear the fog from this confusing topic so that each of you can feel confident on your own unique path.

I take wine for what it really is and talk about what the majority of wine drinkers want to talk about. There are innumerable books about wine, some of them very technical. I don't intend to get overly technical in this book. Wine appreciation needs to be fun and casual, not intimidating. Many of the stories I share in this book come from the most common themes of my recent travels and discussions. I included some history and background information for curious consumers, but if you want to go straight to the practical application stuff and start at part 2, it won't hurt my feelings.

Ultimately, a fine wine is about much more than grape juice. Regardless of when or where—at a cocktail hour, a wedding, a birthday party, or just a dinner with friends and family—wine is shared, and sharing is community.

For me, there is nothing better than watching people raise their glasses, wish each other good health, and enjoy one of my wines. In these moments I feel a great sense of accomplishment for helping to facilitate enjoyment and friendship. I hope that you too feel a sense of community as you learn more about the drink that brings so many people together.

Raise your glass, and let's savor this wine journey together.

HOW I BECAME A WINE PRODUCER

I have had a passion for food and the culinary arts since I was six years old. I had a bad cold, and my mother took me to the doctor. It was in that doctor's waiting room that I came across a cookbook for kids. The book was so simple that there was no real cooking involved, but I was thrilled. When the doctor was ready to see me, I reluctantly put the book back. The entire time I was being examined, all I could think about was that book.

"I really like the cookbook in the waiting room," I finally told the doctor at the end of the checkup. I must have looked very excited, because he laughed.

"Take it with you," he said, patting me on the shoulder. "You can bring it back next time."

"Wow, really? Thanks!" I exclaimed, forgetting about my cold for a moment. Little did I know what that book would spark in me.

It was a couple of days before Valentine's Day, and I had an idea: I was going to cook breakfast for my mom and dad. I couldn't wait. The recipe that caught my interest most, as I flipped through the book in the car, was for french toast. It called for butter, sugar, cinnamon, bread, and one cup of hot water. The only cooking equipment needed was an electric toaster, for which parental supervision was recommended.

As soon as I got home, I made sure we had all the ingredients. I read the recipe over and over to make sure I got it correct. I still remember it. Place the butter in a small bowl with the cinnamon and brown sugar; place that bowl in a larger bowl of hot water until the butter melts; stir the ingredients, spread over toast, and serve. See, I told you it was simple.

The morning of Valentine's Day, I carefully followed the recipe. I was quite proud to enter my parents' room with my culinary creation. Of course, as wonderful parents do, they ate the toast and encouraged me to keep experimenting with new dishes. Although, now that I think about it, I don't recall them asking for seconds.

By the time I was eight years old, I knew that I wanted to be a chef when I grew up—and that's exactly what I did. At seventeen I enrolled in culinary school. For those two years, while I perfected my basic chef skills, I worked in hotels and restaurants. I was a full-time chef and a full-time student, constantly on my feet in hot kitchens, trying to keep my chef coat as clean as possible because I had no time to do laundry.

As part of my first-year culinary course, I couldn't wait for a short semester in wine appreciation. Growing up in the United States is not like growing up in most European countries, where wine is a part of daily life. Many of us had never had wine before, and the professor was going to let us drink in class, even though many of us were underage! We tried mostly French wines, and I was disappointed to find that I didn't like a single one. I was over wine as fast as I was introduced to it. I quickly concluded that wine was not for me. My personal wine journey had begun, and it didn't look as if it was going to go anywhere.

I was led to believe that I would be a full-fledged chef by the time I finished school. Wrong! There is only one thing that can make you a good chef: experience. In order to get that experience, you have to work very hard. And believe me—kitchen labor is not paid well. But I pushed through. By working several jobs at a time, including in large four-star and five-star hotels, I gained experience cooking on the breakfast line, the lunch line, and the dinner line. I worked my way up to the fine-dining kitchen and dabbled in the bakery. I cooked banquets and accepted any challenge offered to me.

Finally, after years of stirring and frying and chopping, I had experience. This meant that I could go virtually anywhere and find a job, since there are restaurants and hotels all around the world. That's exactly what I did: I worked for a hotel chain and looked for transfers to different locations. I was willing to move around as long as I knew I always had a job.

By the age of twenty-four, I had worked full-time in ten hotels and restaurants and part-time in at least a dozen more. I had lived in and cooked in five different US states, the most recent being Colorado, where I was working at the Denver Country Club. I had no clue that my culinary path was about to take a sharp turn.

I was the only person in the kitchen one morning, taking care of some prep work, when the phone rang. I answered it.

"Hello," said a woman with a heavy British accent. "I am looking for James. Is he there?"

"I'm sorry; James no longer works here," I told her. "He left before I started."

She asked me some questions about my career, which I politely answered.

Finally, she explained that she worked for a private placement agency for the elite. "One of my clients is looking for a private chef. Would you be interested in meeting with me to discuss the position?" she asked.

"Of course," I replied. I'm so glad I agreed. A door had opened, and I started cooking privately for the elite. Cooking now became even more fun. Families let me create whatever I wanted. I could explore in ways that many chefs never get to do. I was welcomed into a community of cultured, sophisticated tastes for both food and wine. Money was no object, and only the finer things in life would do.

During this phase of my career I realized that I still hadn't developed a taste for wine. Since my disastrous tasting in culinary school I had tried wine a few times, but I still didn't enjoy it. A fifteen-dollar bottle of wine was too expensive for a beginning chef, and my friends drank beer; it was cheaper and more popular.

The complexity of wine pairing started to become clear to me during my second job as a private chef. My boss had a huge wine cellar full of expensive wines. It was my first week at this new position, and I needed a bottle of wine to make a brown sauce.

"May I take a bottle from the cellar to make the sauce?" I asked my employer (I'll call him Mr. Smith).

He shrugged. "Sure," he said, "as long as you don't use one that's too expensive."

I did not want to show my ignorance, so I just smiled and said okay. I walked into the largest wine cellar I had ever seen, with no clue where to start. There were white wines and red wines; big bottles and small bottles; old wines and new wines; French labels, Spanish labels, Californian labels, and Australian labels. Some wine bottles were in wooden cases; some were wrapped in paper; some were covered in dust and had not been touched in years. I knew better than to use the dusty bottles for cooking.

I had absolutely no idea what to use, so I took a bottle of what he had the most of. I assumed that, since there were so many bottles of this wine, my employer would not miss one. I will never forget the brand or the label: it was a bottle of 1990 Stags Leap from California.

Back in the kitchen, I used about half of the bottle in my sauce and decided to try a little bit of the wine. It wasn't bad. In fact, I liked it.

Maybe all this time I've been missing out, I thought. *Or maybe I like this wine because it is from California. Or maybe this wine is very, very expensive, and that's why I like it. Uh-oh.*

A few minutes later Mr. Smith walked in.

"Which wine did you use?" he asked.

Trying to look nonchalant, I pointed to the bottle.

"That's one of my favorites," he said. "The cases of that particular vintage just arrived a week ago."

"I hope you got a good deal," I said with a nervous laugh.

"I think I did," he said, nodding. "I paid sixty dollars a bottle."

Sixty dollars a bottle! My stomach sank. I could not believe that was the wine I'd grabbed. I felt like such a fool, but I didn't say anything, and neither did he. A few weeks later, I learned this was, in fact, one of the least expensive wines in the cellar at the time. What a relief! Still, sixty dollars a bottle, and that was the cheapest bottle. I was very intrigued. If I liked the sixty-dollar bottle, I thought I would really like the rest of what was in Mr. Smith's cellar. I could only hope that there would be an opportunity to find out.

As time went on, I did get to try more wines, and I started enjoying them. Mr. Smith seemed more comfortable with me picking up ten- to fifteen-dollar wines at the store for cooking, and I tasted them all as I labored in the kitchen. I tried a few ten-dollar bottles for my personal use as well, but I didn't like them. I still didn't appreciate the differences between grape varieties, but I was learning. Most importantly, I was learning about wine and food pairings: big cabernet sauvignons and merlot blends with a nice juicy steak, a pinot grigio with light seafood.

My next chef job was cooking for the "Jones" family. It turned out that my previous experience with Mr. Smith had taught me a lot—enough to teach Mr. Jones. Mr. Jones had a large cellar too. However, he saw no reason to spend more than ten dollars on a bottle of wine, since he could never tell the difference. He was correct not to drink expensive wines he could not appreciate, and he taught me many other lessons I would only later understand.

One day, Mr. Jones invited the French ambassador over for dinner. I knew that the ten-dollar wines in the cellar were not going to do, so I insisted that we up the ante. Mr. Jones hesitantly agreed, and since I was serving the dinner, I enjoyed many compliments on the food and the wine. That very night, even Mr. Jones changed his mind about slightly more expensive wines.

I was now in my midtwenties and had traveled across the United States. I had never left the country before, but I had my passport and was ready to see the world. My girlfriend at the time was offered a job with her company in Chile. The thought of traveling to Chile had never crossed my mind; I had no idea where Chile was, and I did not speak a word of Spanish. But I was in love and believed that I could find a job anywhere. So I thought, *Why not?*

I quickly found a job in a restaurant, and slowly but surely, I started to learn Spanish. But the wonderful experience of living in Chile was at the expense of my own ego. I was embarrassed by my poor Spanish, and I would often tell people, *"Estoy muy embarazada que yo no hablo Castiano muy bien."* I thought I was saying, "I'm very embarrassed that I don't speak Spanish very well."

A few years later, my wife (the same beautiful woman I had moved to Chile with) came home and said, *"Estoy embarazada!"* I could not figure out what she was embarrassed about. Then she told me, in English, that she was pregnant. The look on my face must have been priceless. She asked me why I wasn't excited. The fact is, I had just realized that I had been telling people that I was pregnant for years!

Despite my many humiliating experiences, plenty of good things happened to me in Chile. One of these was meeting a new friend with a great passion for wine and food. Max's attention to the most subtle and delicate flavors just blew my mind. I'll never forget the day we met, about a month after my move. He poured for me a 1997 Miguel Torres sauvignon blanc. It was amazing. I don't know if it was the wine itself, the way Max presented it, or the overall amazing experience of being in Chile.

"Do you taste the notes of straw and grapefruit? And just that touch of asparagus?" he asked in impeccable English.

Asparagus? I thought. That just sounded crazy. I smelled my wine very carefully. "Wow," I said, "I *can* smell asparagus!" The wine instantly became my favorite.

Then we had a chardonnay from a Casablanca winery. Oh my ... notes of apples, coconut, and pineapple. Who knew these aromas truly existed in fermented grape juice? Suddenly, I had a new favorite white wine.

Next was a 1995 Viu Manent Reserva cabernet sauvignon. Oh my goodness, this was amazing. Cherries and spice, with a touch of vanilla. I felt as if I had found the best thing since sliced bread. I finally understood what the world of wine was all about. I wanted to keep trying different wines nonstop, but alcohol finally caught up with me. This is just one reason why wine is a journey, not a destination.

From that day on, my path toward wine appreciation and wine making had begun—and what a fantastic journey it has been. I will always love to cook, but for the past few decades wine has been my life. I have traveled through wine regions in over a dozen countries, taken wine-appreciation courses, and undertaken sommelier training, and for over eleven years I've been making my own Chilean wine, PengWine, with my business partner, Max.

Part I

About Wine

CHAPTER 1

A Brief History of Wine

Who knows how wine really emerged? One wine origin story is about a king and his daughter: the king was mad at his daughter, so the princess planned to kill herself by eating rotten grapes. Instead of getting fatally sick, she felt better after eating the fermented fruit. And now, millennia later, wine makes countless people around the world feel great! How did we get from rotten grapes to delicious bottled wines? It was a long, winding path through numerous countries and wine-making techniques.

It's Good for You

Wine actually started not as a treat but as a necessity. Back when wine was invented, even water could make people sick. Human life spans were not very long until people started boiling water to make coffee and tea. Alcohol kills a lot of contaminants, and very little, if any, bacteria can live in it. This made it the ideal drink, especially for travelers (no, that doesn't mean you should fill your water bottle with wine before your next hike).

This ancient wine probably tasted nothing like what you have in your glass right now. If wine is mishandled, it turns to vinegar; modern winemakers "stabilize" wine so this doesn't happen. In the early days of wine making, no one knew how to do this. Rotting fruit turns to alcohol when left on its own—that's all people knew for centuries. Therefore, the first wines were probably similar to vinegar (yummy). These wines were made and stored in large clay pots, and often spices and herbs were added either for flavor or medicinal purposes.

Vinegar has many health benefits, and the herbs added to its healing properties, but this ancient wine likely wasn't nearly as palatable as what we now enjoy. There was a long, winding journey to get from this acidic mixture to the balanced, aromatic beverage that delights so many drinkers today. And so many different players, from the Greeks and Romans to the Catholics and even French conquerors, contributed to its development.

When in Ancient Rome

Where was the legendary princess when she first ate those fermented grapes? Contrary to what many believe, wine did not originate in France or Italy. It has been traced back to the regions formerly known as Mesopotamia. There is a grape variety referred to by the French as syrah; this grape likely comes from the area of Shiraz in Iraq.[1] If you've seen shiraz wine at your local grocery store, it's because the Australians refer to the syrah grape as shiraz.

While wine may have first appeared in Mesopotamia, the modern wine era started with the Greeks and Romans. The Romans truly perfected the process, though they didn't know exactly how or why at the time. The Romans supposedly stored the clay wine-making vats in torch-lit caves to keep them cool. This technique worked, and it created the tradition of storing wines underground.

More recently, it has been discovered that what was preserving the wines was not so much the cool climate as it was the torches used to light the caves. Lit torches give off sulfur, and sulfur preserves wine.[2] Though sulfur naturally occurs in the wine-making process, additional sulfur is now often added to ensure that wines stay stable and can withstand international shipping.

As the Romans conquered Europe, they brought grapes with them. They planted grapes from Northern Africa all the way to England. Certain grape varieties grew better in different regions because of the climate conditions and the mineral content of the soils. The spread of wine grapes across Europe was one of the most important evolutions in the production, classification, and hierarchy of wine today, because in wine making, location is far more important than wine grape variety. I will return to this concept, referred to as *terroir* (pronounced tehr-wahr), shortly.

Drunk on God

Grapes and wine are hailed in Greek mythology and other ancient cultures and religions. In Greek mythology, Dionysus is the god of the grape harvest, wine making, and wine, as well as ritual madness and ecstasy. The Roman version of this god is Bacchus.

Bacchus and Dionysus were not the real reason wine spread globally. It was Christianity. The Spanish Catholics took grapes to South America and eventually all the way to California. Wine was acceptable among monks and priests, and the best wines in the world were made by monks (Dom Pierre Pérignon, the father of champagne, was a French Benedictine monk). Monks were known for making amazing beers too. I'm sure that, for some people, this was enough reason to become a monk.

Even during the Prohibition era, special licenses were given for wine production for use in ceremonial church activities. Few altar boys admit it, but some of them take their posts because they get to drink wine in the back of the church. I may have been guilty of tasting the wine a few times in my days as an altar boy, but it was only because I didn't want to serve the congregation bad wine!

Conqueror of Wines

There is a common belief, especially in countries relatively new to wine, that the best wines in the world come from France. There is a good historical reason for this. The dominance of French wines was created by none other than Napoleon III. Napoleon requested a classification of wines from a wine-producing region in France known as Bordeaux. The Bordeaux Wine Classification of 1855 defined the hierarchy of today's most prized and pricey wines.[3]

The region of Bordeaux is most recognized for two grape varieties: cabernet sauvignon and merlot (other grape varieties exist there too, such as cabernet franc and petit verdot). The blend of cabernet sauvignon and merlot is the most popular wine blend and is produced all over the world. Napoleon's classification request led to the current wine structure, in which there are five Bordeaux wine producers that are considered the best in France and, quite possibly, the world. The currently recognized five wine houses, known as the First Growth Bordeaux wineries, are Château Lafite Rothschild, Château Margaux, Château Latour, Château Haut-Brion, and Château Mouton Rothschild.[4]

Interestingly, Britain was one of France's first and best customers. The British had such a passion for wine from Bordeaux that the region could not keep up. Newer regions were planted to meet the demand from the thirsty Brits. When Britain and France went to war (and they often did), the British turned to Spain and Portugal for wine. Wine kept British sailors and troops happy during long journeys and battles, and British wine merchants and *négotiants* invented many technological advances in wine production.

Terroir

You may be wondering what makes the wines from the First Growth Bordeaux producers so different from other wines in the world. The grape varieties found in these regions are found throughout most of the wine regions in the world. There are varying wine-making techniques, but many of these are possible to duplicate in different regions and countries. What makes a cabernet sauvignon from France different from a cabernet sauvignon from Chile?

The obvious answer, of course, is where they are grown. A few factors make them taste different, but the most important terroir factors are the land and the microclimate in which the grapes are grown. This is what makes the grapes, and therefore the wines, unique.

Are certain plots of land actually so superior that they mandate thousands of dollars per bottle while wines made right next door only garner a small percentage of that amount? This question can only be answered by those who wish to spend thousands of dollars on a bottle of wine. Personally, I question whether that is the case. I believe that terroir is very important, but I am not convinced that the best plots of land were found hundreds of years ago, especially since entire continents had not even been discovered. With science and technology, combined with the introduction of many new countries to wine making, it is logical to reason that there are many parcels of land in many countries that are just as good, if not better. Regardless, deep-rooted history has had a huge effect on the wine industry. I'm sure the stories of the past will continue to shape wine culture for years to come, for better or for worse.

CHAPTER 2

The Great Grape

The whole world of wine revolves around one tiny, spherical fruit: the grape. I've had many people, especially in countries where wine is just becoming popular, ask me what wine is made out of. The answer is simple: nearly all wines are made from grape juice.

There are innumerable varieties of wine grapes in the world, and each one is unique, with different growing habits and flavors. Winemakers can tell the vines apart by the shape of the leaves, but even that gets a little confusing because grapes easily crossbreed. If one variety is growing on one side of the hill and another variety is growing on the other side of the hill, eventually they start to mingle (just like us humans).

Wine grapes are edible on their own, but table grapes are much better to eat. Seedless table grapes have two to three times the amount of flesh as wine grapes, and they taste less concentrated. Wine grapes are sweet and juicy, but they are also tiny and filled with seeds. Seeds aren't fun to eat; that could be why people decided to make something out of wine grapes instead of eating them. The muscat grape is the one grape that is both a table grape and a wine grape. It's a little bit larger than most wine grapes and is very aromatic.

Grapes may seem simple enough, but there is a lot to know. Which grape varieties make the best wines? Do old vines really make the best fruit? And when are rotting or frozen grapes a good thing? Ladies and gentlemen, welcome to the wonderful, wide, and tasty world of wine grapes.

Red Grapes

Did you know that red grapes are sometimes used to make white wines? In fact, two of the grapes used to make authentic champagne—pinot noir and pinot meunier—are red. How is this possible?

Red and white wines are fermented differently. The juice from most grapes is clear (just think of juice from red table grapes). The color from the skins, when left to ferment with the juice, gives red wine its distinctive hue and flavor. I will go further into the wine-making process later. For now, know that red wines tend to age better than white wines, and they are oaked (aged in oak barrels) more often than white wines. Red wines are commonly blended; it is rare to find a wine that is made from a single red grape, despite what the label may say.

Drink to Your Health

You've probably heard people extol the health virtues of red wine or noticed the many online articles claiming that red wine stops heart attacks? They are talking about resveratrol, a plant compound found in the skins of red grapes. During the process of red wine making, the juice is left in contact with the skins for some time. Thus, red wine contains concentrated amounts of this helpful polyphenol.

Studies have linked resveratrol to a reduced risk of cancer, heart disease, Alzheimer's, and diabetes.[5] But let's not go crazy here. Few studies have used actual people in experiments—most still rely on test tubes and rodents. Experts agree that there is not yet enough evidence to suggest that red wine is the next miracle cure. I have seen such claims as drinking two glasses of red wine is like going to the gym and having a glass of red wine before bed helps reduce your risk of heart disease. While the studies are promising, I believe that the main benefit of a glass of red wine (aside from palate and sensory enlightenment) is happiness.

Most Popular

You will probably recognize some of the names below from stores and wine lists. There are more descriptions of both red and white wine grapes at the back of the book. The pronunciation guides should help you feel more confident the next time you order off a wine menu or go to a tasting.

cabernet sauvignon (cab-ur-nay saw-vee-nyon): One of the most structured, hardy grape varieties. It is a descendant of cabernet franc and is related to sauvignon blanc.

merlot (mehr-low): Please note that, as with many of the French grape names, the *t* is silent. Some people think merlot is the biggest wine, but I think it's the softest. Merlots don't pack a punch like a lot of the other grape varieties. I like more intensity, so I love using merlot in blends.

pinot noir (pea-no nwar): The finickiest, the most passionate, and the most award-winning wine grape. It is the crème de la crème of grapes, but it is also the most stubborn. Every step of the wine-making process is harder with pinot noir. It grows best in cooler climates, and it's hard to ripen and even ferment. But when you get a good one, it is excellent.

sangiovese (sahn-joe-veh-seh): This is the most popular of the multitudinous red Italian grapes. It is frequently used in wines from the Chianti region in Tuscany. Sangiovese wines are fruitier than some other reds and can be oaked or unoaked.

shiraz (shee-raz): Unlike many other types of grapes, shiraz can grow in both warm and cold climates. Shiraz wines can have very different styles and structures depending on where the grapes were grown.

Shiraz was popular in the 1990s and early 2000s, especially in the United States. Australia first put shiraz on the map as a luscious, jam-like, fruity wine. The problem was that, because that formula was so successful, all

Australian shiraz started to taste like overripe fruit bombs. In the past few years, Australia has been more focused on the concept of terroir and distinctive shiraz flavors (a good move in my opinion).

White Grapes

White wines usually (but not always) come from green or white grapes. While they can be cellared, wines made from some grape varieties, like pinot grigio and sauvignon blanc, are typically not made to age for a long time. These wines don't spend much time in barrels and should not be cellared for long either.

White wines, unlike red wines, aren't necessarily blended. There certainly are white blends out there; sémillon, for example, is blended a lot in Australia, and PengWine makes a blend of chardonnay and sauvignon blanc. However, white wines made of a single grape variety are readily available.

Most Popular

chardonnay (shar-doe-nay): Chardonnay grapes make a full-bodied white wine that can be either oaked or unoaked. This grape grows in similar conditions as the pinot noir and is most popular in the French region of Chablis, which mostly grows chardonnay. A number of times people have told me, "I hate chardonnay; I only drink Chablis," which always makes me chuckle.

riesling (reese-ling): A grape variety popular in Germany, riesling is commonly produced in the French region of Alsace. Rieslings can be sweet or dry, and a good riesling can cellar for thirty or forty years. Most wines made with riesling pair very well with spicy food, especially if they have a little bit of sweetness to them.

pinot grigio (pea-no gree-joe): A popular Italian grape variety. It's a very smooth, simple, balanced wine, not too acidic or fruity. Pinot grigio often has a more velvety texture than other white wines. It is not normally cellared, but I have had one or two pinot grigio wines from Australia that were amazing after a decade in the bottle.

sauvignon blanc (saw-vee-nyon blahnk): Sauvignon blanc has a fantastic, dynamic flavor profile. Some people can taste green pepper, capsicum, passion fruit, or lime in these wines. It is usually unoaked, but when oaked, it's often referred to as fume blanc (foo-may-blahnk). Some countries make it smoky, while others keep it very fresh.

Special Wines

There are so many techniques that produce different wines, and they all start in the field. Here are just a few notable ones.

ice wine: Ice wine can be made with just about any grape, but riesling and Vidal are the most popular. The grapes are left on the vine until after the first frost and then are picked and crushed while frozen. The grapes have been on the vine for so long that they are mostly sugar inside, so the resulting wine is very sweet and syrupy.

botrytis wine (bo-try-tiss): Botrytis, also known as noble rot, is a fungus that grows on grapes late in the season. It doesn't mean the grapes have gone bad; instead, it adds a different sweetness and sugar component to the wine. To some people, it tastes like a dessert wine. Want to try it? One of the most famous brands of botrytis wine—one that most wine shops carry—is Noble One from the Yarra Valley in Australia.

Tokaji (toak-eye): This is a type of botrytis wine made in Hungary, originally made for the king of that region. You can spell it *Tokay* or *Tokaji* (Tokaji is the original spelling). Tokaji are very expensive, and some are among the best wines in the world. There are a few dry Tokaji, but they are usually sweet.

fruit wines: Wine can be made from any fruit with high sugar content. There are cherry wines, apple wines, peach wines, mango wines, kiwi wines, and lychee wines. Some winemakers even make combinations, like cabernet sauvignon and blueberry or merlot and raspberry.

port wine: Port wine was created out of necessity. Light, heat, and motion spoil wine. Back in the day, the British were importing wines from France,

Portugal, and Spain on ships, and the rocking of the boats spoiled the wines before they reached their destination. One of the ship captains tried adding brandy to the wine before leaving port, and the fortification kept the wine from spoiling during the journey. Thus, port wine was born.

Just like sparkling wine is only called Champagne if it is made in the Champagne province of France, fortified wine is not called port unless it is made in Douro valley in Portugal. Port wines are usually 15 to 30 percent alcohol and cellar for a very long time. If you want to buy a wine to commemorate a date (like your wedding day or your child's birth year) and save it for a long time, port is a good choice.

Old Vines

Some people think that old vines produce better wine, and that is why the Old World (Europe) produces "better" wine than the New World (anywhere else). How wrong they are. In the mid-1800s, phylloxera—tiny yellow insects—destroyed most of the vineyards in Europe. Many European grapevines needed to be replanted or grafted using rootstocks from the New World. In fact, Chile is the only wine-producing country with no phylloxera, and it has amazing terroir and more-stable weather patterns than much of the Old World. It is Chile, not France, that has many of the oldest original vines in the world.[6]

But, wherever they grow, do older grapevines make better wine? It depends on what you mean by *old*. For most white grape varieties, wine production begins after the vine is about five years old, and at first the wines are just okay. For red grape varieties, vines have to be about seven years old before wine production can begin. The peak is supposedly right around twenty years, and one-hundred-year-old vines are hard to find (kind of like one-hundred-year-old people).

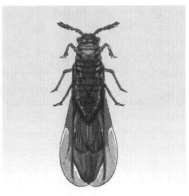

Phylloxera bug

Old vines generally do not produce a lot of fruit, which is one of the reasons people believe old vines are better. In effect, they are self-pruning: many farmers prune plants in order to get larger, quality fruit instead of more lower-quality fruit. Older vines do not need to be pruned, but rather than this being a sign of superiority, I think that the lower yields mean that the vines are struggling to produce fruit in their old age. Just think of an old man with a few hairs left on his head. His lonely hairs are not necessarily better than the hairs on another person's head.[7]

Some wineries prioritize quantity over quality. In fact, a lot of winemakers rip out old vines because they need more fruit or want to plant a different kind of vine.[8] There is a farming reason for doing this as well: crops drain vital nutrients from the soil. This is the reason wheat, corn, peanuts, cotton, and other farmed crops are rotated. Once they've used up all the nutrients in the ground, where are they going to get more? Some winemakers even use cover crops in their vineyards.[9] A cover crop is a crop planted to manage soil erosion, soil quality, water, weeds, and even pests.

So are older vines a sign of better wines? Not necessarily. While a few decades may guarantee a better product, a few centuries certainly don't. A wine made from the fruit of a twenty-year-old vine often trumps a wine made from the fruit of a sixty-year-old vine. There are so many other factors at play that it's hard to justify prioritizing vine age over all the rest.

The Fruit That Started It All

Grapes, in all their varieties and growing conditions, are at the heart of the wine industry. And all these grapes—white, red, fungus-infested, frozen, or otherwise—eventually find their way into cool cellars and onto store shelves. How do we get from ripe fruit to a delicious bottle of wine? Pour yourself a glass and read on to find out!

CHAPTER 3

From Vine to Wine:
The Wine-Making Process

This is where the true art begins. There are countless variables in wine making, and every single one counts. First, there is the grape variety and the location of the vineyard. Then there is the method of harvest, as well as the exact day and even *hour* of harvest. Then there is fermentation, pressing, aging, and all the minute details involved. There's little wonder that, with so many factors at play, no two wines taste exactly the same.

Red or White? It's All in the Process

You already know that red grapes can make white wine. This is because red grape juice is clear—it is the skins of red grapes that give red wines their color. Remove the skins fast enough, and the juice stays clear.

Red wine is made using the must (pulp) of red grapes. The juice is fermented with the grape skins, and the wine is pressed after fermentation is complete. At that point, the skins have dyed the juice red.

During white wine making, the grapes are crushed or pressed straightaway, and the skins are discarded. The immediate separation prevents the grape skins from dying the juice red, making wines like champagne possible.

Growing Conditions

Remember the concept of terroir? Winemakers are obsessed with it because the flavor of the wine doesn't start in the winery; it starts in the vineyard. In fact, the vineyard is the most important part of making great wine. The location, soil, and weather shape the finished wine in unpredictable ways.

One day at PengWine, for instance, we got everything set up out in our vineyard for an outdoor blend tasting session. Some visitors from the United States joined us, excited to help with our new blends. Right when we were about to start, a huge wall of smoke rolled in, and we had to cancel the session. It turned out that a farmer just down the road was burning eucalyptus scraps. Eucalyptus has a very intense scent, and it landed on our grapes. There was nothing we could do about it.

Thanks to the farmer down the road, some of our vintages now have distinctive eucalyptus flavors. I like it. It just goes to show that anything and everything affects wine. I can smell my vineyard even in vintages unaffected by wafting eucalyptus, and when I smell other wines, I can't help but think of the vineyards they came from.

Harvest Time

HOW TO MAKE RED WINE

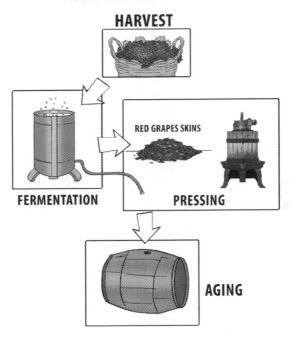

Grape harvests are all about timing. Earlier grapes have less sugar, more acidity, and a greener, harsher tannin. Later grapes have more sugar, less acidity, and softer tannins.

Once it's time to harvest, wineries can use either manual labor or machines. Premium wines are made of only the best bunches, and currently that kind of harvest can only be done by hand. Winemakers that use harvesting machines believe that machines do a better job; I've gotten into lots of arguments about this. The problem is that machines are not selective, and I'm not just talking about fruit. Human harvesters need light, so they must work during the day. Machine harvesting is done at night because of the cooler temperatures, which encourage sugar concentration in fruit. And in the dark, anything can fall off the vine. I've seen birds, rats, mice, spiders, and all sorts of other things get caught in the harvesting bin. Whatever goes in the bin—plants and animals alike—can end up fermenting in the tank.

Now, don't let this put you off of drinking machine-harvested wines (you might get one rat for every ten thousand bunches of wine). The point is that this is possible with machine harvesting. If people are handpicking grapes, they aren't likely to pluck a rat off the vine and place it into the harvesting bin. I believe in hand harvesting, but I also think that it doesn't make a huge difference, especially with less expensive wines.

Squeeze Those Grapes

As I mentioned before, the pressing process occurs at different times for white and red wines. White wine grapes are pressed right after harvesting, while red wine grapes are pressed after fermentation. Whenever pressing happens, it involves interesting equipment ranging from medieval to modern. Pneumatic presses, a more recent invention, have large balloons inside them; the balloons fill up with air and press the grapes against the side of the tank. In basket presses, a big metal press smashes the grapes down into a basket. Some wineries still do things the old-fashioned way— their employees jump in and crush the grapes by foot (wearing protective footgear, of course). I've even seen large wooden presses operated by horses!

The amount of pressure exerted by the press affects the intensity of the juice. Just imagine the kind of juice you would get from lightly squeezing a fruit versus smashing it to pieces. Many wineries press the juice in stages, keeping the different juices separate for different batches of wine.

Juice Flows

1. Free-flow juices	Little to no pressure	Clear juice
2. First press	Light pressure	Clear juice
3. Second and third press	Medium to heavy pressure	Clear to opaque, depending on the style of wine

First are the free-flow juices, which need only a light touch to emerge. Some wineries use the weight of the grapes piled on top of each other to get the free-flow juices. Then comes the first pressing, released with gentle pressure. The second and third pressings are much more intense.

Free-flow and first-press juice is normally quite clear. But after the second and third presses, more color starts to appear. The skins of the grapes react more with heavier pressing, creating stronger flavors. In red wine production, everything—the grapes, skins, and juice—are left in the press for a while, and the juice and the skins mingle to create the flavor and body of the wine. Depending on the wine style, this takes anywhere from a day to several months.

From Juice to Wine

After the grapes have been thoroughly squished, the juice is separated from the skins and stabilized to prepare for fermentation. This is the part that splits regular old grape juice from wine. For both red and white wines, yeast—the tiny organisms responsible for so many wonderful foods and drinks, including bread and beer—fuels fermentation. Wineries either add yeast or let natural yeast materialize in the juice. Many winemakers now induce the wine with a specific strand of yeast.

During fermentation, the yeast eats sugar and creates alcohol (wouldn't it be nice if we could do that?), carbon dioxide, and heat. The amount of sugar in the grape depends on how much sunshine the grape got. The more sun, the more sugar; the more sugar, the more alcohol. As the fermentation process gives off heat, the wine starts to "cook."

Yeast is most active at warmer temperatures, and if it gets cold enough, it becomes dormant (just think of bread dough: if you freeze it, it does not rise). The ideal temperature for fermenting wine is about 62 degrees Fahrenheit. In certain wineries fermentation takes place in the fall, and if it gets too cold, the yeast stops reacting to the sugar. This results in a "stuck fermentation," which is a winemaker's worst nightmare. The wine has to stay just hot enough until the winemaker chooses to stop fermentation.

Some winemakers ferment their wine in oak barrels (they think this extracts a different oak flavor than usual oak aging). Some wineries let slightly crushed grapes barrel ferment, skins and all. But barrel fermentation is a time-consuming method, and it's very expensive. Most wineries, including PengWine, ferment in stainless steel instead and save the barrels for aging.

Fermenting can finish within a few weeks depending on the volume of the wine. Barrel fermentation usually takes slightly longer than stainless steel fermentation. In either case, by the time fermentation is finished, the juice has miraculously become wine. Thanks, yeast!

A Good Kind of Aging

Aging adds depth and character to the wine and takes a lot longer than fermenting. Barrel aging can take one month to several years. The fermentation process changes a wine's chemical composition, and the aging process continues to alter it. I could get very technical here, but I don't want to bore you. Suffice it to say that aging makes a wine taste smoother by slowly mellowing harsh flavors, acids, and tannins.

Oak Aging

Oak aging is popular in the wine industry because of the distinctive flavor profile it creates. But be careful when exploring oaked wines: a lot of people have undiagnosed allergies to oak. I am allergic to oak, and I just found out last year! If you get a headache after drinking oak-aged wines, you might want to get an allergy test.

A fun fact about oak barrels: an oak barrel only works well three times. After that, it's just a holding device that lets wine breathe. I have no idea why, but the first time a barrel is used, it is called *new oak*, the second time is called *first use*, and the third time is called *second use*. Therefore, a barrel being used a second time is on its "first" use. Is that confusing or what?

Wine barrels can be made from other types of wood besides oak but they probably shouldn't be. Getting oak from Europe to South America in the 1700s and 1800s wasn't possible for Chilean winemakers, so they used wood from the rauli tree to make barrels instead. Some wineries are now bringing it back, but I think there's a reason it fell out of style. According to old reports, rauli gave wines an unpleasant musky flavor.[10] To make matters worse, rauli barrels didn't even last as long as oak barrels.[11] Considering that, I am not about to start aging my wines in rauli barrels. In this case, European tradition wins.

Wood

The top four oak-barrel-producing countries are the United States, France, Hungary, and China. Why? There are no Southern Hemisphere countries that produce an oak that is dense enough to store liquid! The trees there just don't get as big as the trees in the Northern Hemisphere.

Just as wine starts in the vineyard, barrels start in the forest. Believe it or not, flavor profiles produced by oak barrels vary drastically depending on where the wood is from. An American oak typically adds more coconut and vanilla flavors, while French oaks exude more spice flavors. PengWine barrels cost €1,000 because they are from the best forest in the best barrel-producing region of France. American oak barrels, on the other hand, cost about $200.

China started producing barrels a few years ago. They have always had dense oak trees, but the negative "Made in China" connotation hasn't done the industry any favors. It's too bad, because Chinese oak barrels produce good flavor. Some of my winemaker friends have experimented with Chinese oak and gotten very good results, but no one has used it enough to isolate a specific flavor profile yet.

Forged in Flames

There is more to a barrel than the wood from which it was made. Some barrels are charred, or "toasted," on the inside with an open flame. There are light-, medium-, and heavy-toasted barrels, and the level of toasting impacts the flavor of the wine. There are also different parts of the barrel that can be toasted; sometimes the heads (ends) of the barrels are toasted, whereas other times only the inner staves are toasted.

As with other products, size and make matter. Handmade barrels, crafted by professional coopers, are much nicer and far more expensive than manufactured barrels. Barrel size impacts the flavor of the wine, since a larger surface area creates a more heavily oaked wine. The average oak barrel is 225 liters. We at PengWine use hogs (300-liter barrels) to get maximum oak flavor.

Knock It Off

Putting oak staves into stainless steel fermentation tanks, while not very refined, is the cheapest way to add oak flavor to a wine. But some wineries won't even invest in real oak staves—they would rather go to great lengths to trick customers. Some buy old oak barrels, turn them into sawdust, and sprinkle the dust onto their wine. There are even wineries that add liquid oak, the oak equivalent of imitation vanilla extract. Wineries tell customers that all these wines are oak aged, and the only way to tell is to have a taste. If you think that's messed up, wait until you get to the next chapter, where I will discuss more eccentricities of the wine industry.

Blends

As I mentioned before, almost every red wine is a blend, even though the wine bottle doesn't say so. This is because red wines made from a single grape variety are just plain boring. Wineries know this, but they don't want to confuse consumers, and they aren't under obligation to tell consumers which grapes they use. A bottle might say cabernet sauvignon, but it may be 25 percent merlot, which is for the best. I wouldn't pick up a glass of merlot, but I would definitely go for a glass of cabernet sauvignon and merlot.

Even though the combinations aren't usually disclosed, many of the best wines in the world are blends. Bordeaux—a region where one bottle of wine might cost €1,000—exclusively produces blended wines. Bordeaux is restricted by law to growing cabernet sauvignon, merlot, cabernet franc, petit verdot, and malbec. Consumers know that Bordeaux wines can only contain these varieties, but the winemakers don't have to tell the consumer the exact ratios.

At PengWine, we think our customers deserve to know what they are drinking, so we put the blends right on the labels. Every year the blend changes; it could be 60 percent to 40 percent one year and 70 percent to 30 percent the next. It all depends on what blend tastes best that particular year.

Vintage

If I had a penny for every time someone asked me about vintages, I'd have a copper mine. Sometimes I wonder if people care about vintages or if they just think it's a smart thing to ask about. The truth is that vintages matter much less than people expect.

During a vintage year, growing conditions are optimal. There was just the right number of hot days, cold nights, and rainy afternoons for the vines to flourish. There were no frosts early in the growing season. In many European countries, growing conditions vary year after year, and vintage is therefore important. In countries like Chile, the United States, and New Zealand, weather patterns are more consistent, and thus the vintages don't vary as much. In these countries it makes more sense to keep track of bad years, since good years are the norm.

The vintage on the label of a wine bottle usually corresponds to the year the grapes were harvested. For the most part, each country has firm laws about what percentage of the wine in the bottle must be from the specified year. In some countries, 85 percent of the wine must be from a single vintage in order to be labeled as such; other countries have a 75 percent policy. These rules are enforced more in the Old World wine regions. There are also many nonvintage wines, especially sparkling wines and Champagne. These wines, including PengWine Emperor Wine, are intentionally made from multiple vintages.

It is true that older wines have a story (or stories) to tell. Take 2010, for example. In Chile, this was a very challenging vintage. The growing conditions were fantastic, but a week into the red grape harvest there was an earthquake measuring 8.8 on the Richter scale. This caused havoc, and the wine industry was heavily affected. Barrels and tanks were destroyed, and bottles of wine were smashed on the floors of many cellars. Many wines from 2008 and 2009 were lost.

Fortunately, PengWine suffered very little damage from the earthquake. That is not to say we were unscathed. The handpicking of the 2010 vintage was abandoned as workers attended to those in need. Every time I drink a 2010 wine from Chile, I think about the intensity of that quake and the impact it had on so many lives.

And yet the story a wine tells may not even be about the winemaker, the region, or the winery. It could just be about you. Perhaps 2010 was a wonderful year for you, and the thought of that year always brings about wonderful memories. I love coming across wines from 1999 because I got married that year. In fact, as a wedding present I gave my wife a case of 1999 wine bottles to open each year on our anniversary. Some of them have aged well, others not so well.

As far as very old wines go, they can be very good, but they are not *necessarily* good. Much of it is a marketing ploy. If someone pours you a glass of wine and tells you it is from 1950, you probably won't dare tell them it tastes terrible. But if it's bad, it's bad. People cling to the mythic belief that older wine is better, but it is important to hold old wines to the same standards as any other wine. This is especially true because, in 99 percent of cases, vintage does not matter at all (as you are about to learn).

The Slow and Fast of It

Wine is a lot like food in some ways. Fast food is made on a massive scale, and consistent flavor and cheap prices are priorities. "Slow food" focuses on the best of everything: superior ingredients, preparation, and recipes. There is also everything in between: food that is neither fast nor slow, pretty good but not gourmet. Here's how these categories apply to our favorite beverage.

	Slow wines	Standard wines	Fast wines
Price	$30+	$10–$30	Less than $10
Age	5+ years	1–5 years	Less than 1 year
Fun fact	Less than 1 percent of wines are slow wines	Standard reds are best if they are over a year old	Vintages on fast wines are like expiration dates

Slow Wines

Slow wines are the wines you find in nice restaurants and wine cellars. They are carefully and traditionally made, and they have the price tags to prove it. This is the only wine category where vintage really matters. Slow wines age gracefully, developing more complexity over time. The aging process could take a few years or a few decades, depending on the winemaker's techniques. The region of Champagne, for instance, may not release a vintage until it is a decade old.

A quality winemaker considers what may happen to a wine after years of cellaring during the production process. When a wine that has been sitting for years is finally opened, it can be a winemaker's most gratifying or crushing moment. I always feel nervous and excited when I open a vintage of my own and relieved if it turned out well.

Wine aficionados obsess over slow wines as much as foodies obsess over farm-to-table restaurants. The exact growing conditions for slow wines are common knowledge in the industry. People delight in comparing different vintages from the same vineyard or comparing slow wines from the same region.

Standard Wines

According to *Wine Enthusiast Magazine*, about 90 percent of wines are consumed within forty-eight hours of purchase.[12] It is clear, therefore, that people are not buying wines to keep them for years. With this in mind, many wines are made to last only five years in the bottle. These are what I call standard wines—still made well but not the best of the best.

Most white wines—riesling, pinot grigio, sauvignon blanc—are not made to cellar for a long time anyway, so you can purchase an excellent standard white wine. If the vintage year on a standard red wine is the current year, though, go for something else. Most decent red wines in this category need to age a little.

When selecting a vintage for a standard wine, keep in mind that the grape harvest is February through June in the Southern Hemisphere and August through October in the Northern Hemisphere. Therefore, wines from the Southern Hemisphere are at least six months older than wines from the Northern Hemisphere with the same vintage year.

Fast Wines

Fast wines start with the cheapest grape juice in existence. Manufacturers ferment it, and as soon as it turns to alcohol, they carbonate it, modify it, augment it, bottle it, and sell it. Just like in the fast-food industry, there is lots of manipulation involved in fast wines. They are produced like any other mass-produced soft drink or beverage and are designed to taste the same year after year, regardless of growing conditions, with the help of additives.

Fast wines are made to be consumed within a year or two and will not get better with age. The vintage year on a fast wine is more of an expiration date than it is a sign of quality or distinction. Additionally, if wine gives you headaches, don't drink wines from this category. Just like fast food, fast wines contain lots of chemical additives and stabilizers that don't sit well with some folks.

That said, if you simply want to taste different grape varieties, fast wines should deliver. Like fast food, they can also be fun to indulge in once in a while. One excellent example of a fast wine is Beaujolais nouveau, a French fast wine named for its home region. This red wine is made from gamay grapes and is fermented just a few weeks before it is sold. Thanks to a clever marketing tactic in the 1950s, races are now held to get bottles of Beaujolais nouveau to different places around the world—Europe, Asia, and North America—the third week of November each year. Fireworks, parties, and plenty of cheap wine complete the festivities.[13] But Beaujolais nouveau goes bad quickly; if you still have it by the following spring, throw it away.

Old World, New World

By now you have seen the terms *Old World wines* and *New World wines* quite a few times. I've never liked these categories, but because they are an industry standard, I should probably accept them. There are many misconceptions about the difference between the two, though. First of all, to put one matter to rest, neither category is better than the other. Secondly, the vines from the Old World, thanks to phylloxera, are not actually older than the vines of the New World. There are some vines in the Old World that are older, but there are many original vines in the New World that are older than those in the Old World. There are, however, some true distinctions between the two categories. Here's what you need to know.

Old World and New World Wines

	Old World	New World
Where	Europe	Everywhere else
Flavor	Earthy	Fruity
Method	Traditional	Modern
Focus	Terroir	Grape variety
Label	Region	Grape variety
Alcohol	Lower	Higher

Old World

European regions such as Italy, France, Spain, Portugal, Germany, and Hungary are all in the Old World. Generally, if a wine is a bit more earthy or farm-like in flavor, it is Old World. Many believe that the Old World uses more-traditional techniques in their wine-making process and therefore create smaller, more-expensive batches of wine.

The Old World is more focused on terroir than the grape variety. Old World wines are labeled based on regions; oftentimes the grape variety is not even listed on the bottle. This is because each region can only legally grow certain grape varieties.

New World

New World areas are all other wine-producing regions. The United States, Australia, New Zealand, Chile, Argentina, and South Africa all fall into this category. Wine labeling in these regions is based first on grape variety, second on region. As parts of the New World started focusing on terroir, there have been some shifts toward smaller regions and subregions, but overall grape variety still reigns.

In general, New World wineries use more technology (with the exception of Beaujolais nouveau, most fast wines are New World wines). The flavor profile is also different: if a wine is fruity and sweet, it is probably New World. The alcohol content of New World wines is usually higher than that of Old World wines, simply because New World wineries tend to get more sun.

One World?

The tradition-steeped Old World has experienced winemakers using historically proven techniques. However, the growing conditions of the New World are slightly better than those of the Old World. While it is true that most low-quality wines are produced in the New World, some New World wines are phenomenal.

I think production fundamentals are generally the same for well-made wines, no matter where they are from. I look at it this way: if a factory makes lots of food, it likely needs a laboratory, whereas a restaurant does not. But the factory owner can choose to use great care in making the products or can choose to cut corners at the expense of the products. Without a doubt, there is just as much fast food out there as there is fast wine. But that doesn't mean that there isn't plenty of excellent food—and excellent wine—in the New World.

From Vine to Bottle

Whether grapes come from a premium winery in Bordeaux or a massive farm in California, the basic process is the same. Whether the grapes are merlot, carmenére, or pinot grigio, the basic process is the same. Wherever they are and whatever variety they are, those grapes are harvested, crushed, and fermented into a liquid that lines grocery store shelves and restaurant wine cellars all over the world. But the bottles that hold that liquid—and what their labels say—have a whole other story.

CHAPTER 4

Don't Judge a Wine by Its Label

People don't buy ugly things. This is true of so many products, and wine is no different. The label, stopper, and even the wine's position on the shelf can all influence sales, no matter how delicious (or horrible) the wine actually is. And even if you want to know what's inside the bottle, the label usually won't tell you.

Wine Distribution

The wine and spirits industry is very complex. Before a bottle of wine is placed before you, it goes through many trials and tribulations, some of them necessary and some of them decidedly unnecessary. If you buy a bottle of wine that is not local, it has likely gone through an importer. In many countries, wine goes from the importer to the distributor and then to the retailer, who sells it to you.

Who profits from all the bureaucracy? Not me! The average winery in the world earns less than 3.9 percent profit per year. The importers, distributors, retailers, and other players make more than the producers because that's just the way the wine world works.

What's on the Label?

I've already discussed the difference between Old World and New World wine labeling. The real trouble comes not with what is on the label but with what isn't on the label. An importer can represent one winery or dozens of wineries, and each winery could have dozens of labels. Wineries can split labels between a few different importers, complicating things further. More and more wineries now bottle the same wine under different labels and then sell the bottles at different prices. This bothers me very much, but it is the state of the industry.

Some wines with nearly identical labels and vintages taste very different depending on where they are sold. They are clearly different wines sold in the same bottles. It is fine to create wines with different profiles, but they should be labeled differently! And believe it or not, these are just a few of the deceptive practices used by the wine industry.

Added Wine Ingredients

A top wine buyer once asked me, "How much blueberry, chocolate, and spice do you put in the wine? Is that what makes it more expensive?" It dawned on me then that many people don't know that wine is supposed to be made from just grapes.

Wineries shouldn't use any additives to enhance the aroma or taste. They shouldn't, but that doesn't mean that they don't. Why aren't wine ingredients listed on the back of the bottle? One can assume that wine is just made from grapes, right? But think about this: beer lists ingredients. Every other processed food item in the world lists the ingredients. Even *water* lists the mineral contents on every bottle! Yet no such regulation exists for wine and spirits. Even Irish cream does not list the ingredients, and who knows what's in that?

The unregulated, bastardized state of the wine industry drives me nuts. In most countries, wine labels only have to specify alcohol content and whether the wine is white or red (for which there is no detailed definition). Some countries require a warning about the adverse effects of alcohol, especially for drivers and pregnant women. But perhaps all foods labels should mention that eating too much causes drowsiness and weight gain.

In 2015, a class action lawsuit was filed in the United States that highlighted wine labeling issues. The suit against many producers of cheap wines (including flipflop, Franzia, and Charles Shaw) materialized because these wines contain high levels of inorganic arsenic. The cheaper the wine, the higher the level of arsenic. Do you think that is a coincidence? And where did the arsenic come from: the farm, the pesticides, or the additives?[14] I think consumers at least deserve to know if they are drinking additives and arsenic.

Sulfites

Wine labels sometimes mention a single additive: sulfites. You may have noticed this on the back of wine labels, and you may have even heard people complain about getting headaches from wine with added sulfites.

Despite the rumors, sulfites are usually nothing to worry about. Sulfur dioxide ($SO2$) is a naturally occurring gas, a component of most fruits, and a natural byproduct of the wine-making process. Recall that the use of added sulfur dioxide in wine making started with the Romans, who unknowingly preserved their wines by burning torches in their underground wine cellars. Today, winemakers still sometimes add extra sulfites to wine to stabilize it and prepare it for shipping and prolonged cellaring,

Sulfur dioxide can have some adverse effects if inhaled. I have even seen people get light-headed from standing near the buckets of grape stems, which exude some sulfur dioxide. People with asthma are extra sensitive to sulfites and may want to take appropriate precautions.[15] However, many foods contain sulfites, and most people do not even notice. In fact, a small box of raisins has much more sulfur than an entire bottle of wine. So unless raisins give you headaches, the sulfites in wine are probably not responsible for your wine-induced complaints.

The French Standard

Some countries have caught on to this problem and now require strict testing on imported wines. I've noticed that countries that are not big wine producers have the strictest standards. Countries that don't screen wines, on the other hand, are filled with subpar and potentially dangerous products.

Although it is a big wine producer, France (not surprisingly) has the most thorough and most enforced wine production regulations. Each region has slightly different regulations, and guidelines ensure that wines are an artistic expression of a region, a winemaker, and Mother Nature rather than a cocktail of undisclosed ingredients. The addition of water, sugar, or any flavorings is strictly regulated in most regions. In some French areas, winemakers cannot even manually water the grapes during the growing season.

These rules and regulations can make it very difficult for wine producers to be competitive. Given the extremes of climate change, some regions are tweaking their rules. But even so, the French rules are enforced, and there are strict penalties for breaking them. Thank goodness someone sets standards!

Organic and Biodynamic Wines

You may have noticed more organic and biodynamic wines appearing on store shelves lately. Organic or biodynamic wines are often higher quality than your average fare; if a winery goes through the trouble of getting one of these qualifications, it produces a cleaner product. But what is the difference between these biodynamic and organic wines, anyway?

Organic and biodynamic wines are actually pretty different. Organic wine is made with grapes that have not been treated with chemicals. The wine also does not have any added inorganic ingredients. But how far does this go? Does this mean that the barrels are organic too? Not usually.

Biodynamic wines go a step further. In addition to adhering to organic requirements, biodynamic fertilizers come from animals that live at the vineyard. The grapes are also treated and harvested according to a strict lunar calendar. There are pluses and minuses to biodynamic wines. The process is very meticulous and standards are set high, but some winemakers find biodynamic requirements restrictive.

Should you choose biodynamic or organic wines over other wines? Not necessarily. Many slow and standard wines are created organically, even if they aren't labeled as such. But if you prefer to eat only organic, you may want to avoid fast wines the same way you avoid fast food.

Awards

Have you ever seen a sticker on a bottle that looks like an award? Winemakers know that award-winning wines garner higher prices, so they add extra stickers or seals to their bottles. Luckily, if you pay attention, you can tell which awards are legitimate and which ones mean absolutely nothing.

Is a ten-dollar wine with a gold medal better than a twenty-dollar wine without a medal? Be careful. Remember that winemakers can create their own contests and give themselves oddly specific awards. You could award yourself first place in a Person with My DNA Sequence World Championship if you wanted to. The wine with a gold medal may be the only wine that was entered into a particular event. It may have earned an award specific to one region or grape variety. As you might guess, a merlot that won an award at a merlot-only event is not necessarily better than the cabernet beside it.

I have seen round gold stickers on wines that hadn't even been entered into contests. Some wineries decorate their bottles with decals that look incredibly similar to awards, knowing most people won't look closely enough to tell the difference. A few years back I came across a bottle with a round gold sticker that said, "Best enjoyed with *Seinfeld*." It was surprisingly good, even without *Seinfeld*—but it certainly wasn't an award-winning wine.

Stoppers

You probably know that many wines are enclosed with cork, and likely you have seen wines with screw caps or fake corks as well. While cork has been used for generations, synthetic cork and screw caps are both relatively new to the wine world, and some people aren't welcoming the change. Are corks really superior, or is a bottle of wine with a screw cap just as good?

The History of Stoppers

Cork Tree

One of my favorite stories is that of the discovery of Champagne. Before corks, rags or pieces of fabric were used to stopper bottles. The bottles were dipped in wax to seal the openings. Rags are not great enclosures for wine; they allow air to get into the bottles, even with wax seals. One day, a blind monk named Dom Pérignon was tasting his latest batch of wine when he noticed a bubbly sensation: carbonation created by the fermentation and air exposure. He said, "Come, my brothers, for I am drinking stars!" This began the intentional production of Champagne as we know it today.

Although fabric bottle stoppers helped to create the first Champagne, cork is a much better enclosure for wine. It's nostalgic, romantic, and practical. Remember, a fine wine is alive and is always changing in the bottle. Cork allows a wine to age well, expanding and contracting ever so slightly while keeping oxygen out.

The cork tree grows in many places in the world, but many wine-producing regions cannot produce cork trees hearty enough to make wine corks. The cork used for enclosing wine bottles is best sourced from Portugal and Spain. The actual cork part of the tree is the bark. After the cork is harvested, the tree grows the bark back and is ready for another harvest in about nine years. In my opinion, this is good for the environment. The more trees we plant and cultivate, the better!

A few decades ago, cork wasn't so popular. It was being blamed for corked wines, which, while safe to drink, tend to taste like cardboard. Cork taint is usually caused by a chemical called trichloroanisole (TCA), which was long believed to exist only in corks. However, recent studies show that TCA can also be found in barrels and other parts of the wine-making process. Many wineries have tried plastic or synthetic corks and even screw caps to minimize the possibility of cork taint, but in reality, a bottle of wine with a screw cap can still be corked.

Regardless, the fear of cork taint (combined with the fact that many wine makers did not like paying high prices for Spanish and Portuguese cork) made synthetic corks all the rage. Many new synthetic cork producers started touting how much better synthetic corks are than actual corks. After about five years, the touting stopped, and many wineries had to dump out case after case of spoiled wine. It turned out that many synthetic corks ruin fine wines after a few years. Synthetic corks are good for wines consumed within two years, but that's about it.

The rise and fall in the popularity of synthetic corks caused a ripple effect. For a time, many producers stopped buying real cork and switched to the cheaper and supposedly better synthetic cork. Demand for real cork fell sharply. The economy was already bad in Spain and Portugal, and many of the farms were sold and turned into real estate developments. As wine producers returned to real cork, prices spiked, and a cork shortage ensued.

With a scarcity of real cork and skyrocketing production costs, the industry needed a new solution. The screw cap became more popular and was eventually touted even more than the synthetic cork that came before it.

I'll never forget when screw caps first started appearing on decent wines. It was 2007, and I decided that I had better try a few screw-cap wines before I made any judgment. I purchased a couple of twenty-dollar screw-cap bottles of wine and placed them in my wine cellar. I had never had a wine with a screw cap in the house before.

One night, I was out, and my wife was hosting a dinner party at home. When I got home, I found all my cork pullers on the countertop. There were about five waiter's-friend corkscrews (two of which were broken), a deluxe Screwpull-R, a hand cork puller, an electric cork puller, a gas cork pusher, and every other cork puller we owned. Beside them were three bottles of wine, the tops of which were completely torn to pieces. I stood there in complete disbelief, wondering what had happened. Then it occurred to me: someone at the dinner party had never seen a wine with a screw cap, and they certainly hadn't expected to find wines with screw caps in my house! It turned out that that someone was my wife, who knew that I was skeptical about the screw cap at the time and was unaware of my purchase. And of course, now we are comfortable with screw caps.

Which One Is Best?

The jury is still out on which stoppers are best for wine; only time will tell. But the cork and screw cap each have their place in the market. Though some say the screw cap is great for aging wine, I don't agree. Screw caps don't ruin wine like synthetic corks do, but cork still does a better job. I think the screw cap is good for standard and fast wines, but I really love the sound of a popping cork coming from a nice bottle of wine.

In hotels and other establishments where large volumes of wine are used, the screw cap is much more convenient than cork. If it takes one minute to open a bottle with a cork and one hundred bottles are needed for an event, opening them all takes nearly two hours. It takes only a few seconds to unscrew a cap, and I can understand why the hotel industry prefers that.

The screw cap has some disadvantages too. The wine industry did not expect people to exploit the screw tops by opening bottles of wine before buying them. Some people twist the top off, take a swig, and decide if the wine is worth the twenty-dollar price tag. Always check the seal of a screw-top bottle of wine before you buy it to make sure someone hasn't already had a taste.

Packaging

The wine industry is devoted to creative packaging. Fermented grape juice comes in containers of all shapes, sizes, and materials. Wine is sold in juice boxes and individually sealed wineglasses. If you love a wine enough, you can buy it by the barrel. Though the wine bottle is the traditional choice, even that has many forms; the piccolo bottle contains only 187 milliliters (0.187 liters) of liquid, while the Nebuchadnezzar holds 15 liters.

Cheaper wine is sometimes sold in boxes, cartons, and cans. But on the other end of the spectrum, a big competition is taking place. Walk through any duty-free airport shop, and you could see leather boxes, crystal bottles, backpacks, roller bags, ice buckets, and picnic baskets filled with wine. They all try to stand out in the crowd, screaming, "Choose me, choose me!"

Let me be clear: a big, heavy bottle and a wooden crate do not guarantee a good bottle of wine. In fact, the bag-in-box packaging, though typically used for cheap wines, is the best and most consistent wine storage vessel. The bag does not affect the taste of the wine, and air cannot enter the bag as the wine is poured. Thus, the last glass is as fresh as the first one. The only problem is that people think that boxed wines are terrible, so even a quality boxed wine is hard to sell.

My biggest pet peeve about organic and biodynamic wines is the packaging. Picking up a bottle of organic or biodynamic wine and nearly breaking my arm from the sheer weight of the packaging is infuriating. Why does this drive me mad? Think about all the effort winemakers expend to protect the environment during the entire wine-making process. Then, once the wine is finished, they create a giant carbon footprint by choosing the heaviest packaging possible.

It's the Inside That Counts

Though many producers dress their wines up with fancy leather boxes and superfluous awards, in the end it's the inside that counts. Although a pretty bottle might entice buyers, the contents of the bottle keep buyers coming back for more. It should go without saying that if a wine is very cheap, there is a reason. Think about a wine that costs just a few dollars. How much do the cork, bottle, label, and shipping box cost? Add in the cost of shipping and the profit margins of the importer, distributor, and retailer. What does that leave for the actual production cost of the wine? All this and they still don't have to put the ingredients on the label. Does anyone still think that fast wines are just pure fermented grape juice?

It is more labor intensive to pick grapes by hand. Storing a wine in an oak barrel for eighteen months costs more than spiking it with liquid oak extract. And of course, volumes are much lower when wines aren't watered down. But although they usually can't pour money into packaging, many smaller producers stick to French standards. These winemakers aren't looking for shortcuts; they make wine because they love the process and the product.

A revolution is already under way in the food industry. Many consumers demanded transparency, saw what was wrong with the food production process, and changed the way that they ate. Such a revolution is long overdue in the wine industry. As a producer (and, of course, a consumer) of wine, I hope it is just around the corner. I hope that wine drinkers see the hard work and dedication it takes to produce quality wine and seek more clarity in the industry. When they do, I think they will gladly pay a bit more to support smaller producers and help keep the more traditional styles of wine making alive.

PART II

BUYING WINE

CHAPTER 5

So You Know What You Like:
Isn't That Enough?

When I was in culinary school, I hated expensive French wines—and it wasn't my fault. No one should ever start with expensive French wines. If you are new to alcohol (or just to wine), you won't be able to detect many of the subtleties that excite connoisseurs. Even if you have been drinking wine for a while, everyone's taste buds are different, and yours may not favor certain types of wine. By following the advice in this chapter, you can develop your own wine palate and find lots of new wines to try and love.

Alcohol Burn: Wine for New Drinkers

I now understand why I didn't like wine when I was seventeen years old. It had nothing to do with region or grape variety. It was the same thing that plagues many young wine drinkers: alcohol burn. If you have been drinking alcohol for a few years, think back to when you first started. You probably enjoyed mixed drinks (the sweeter, the better). I have been training waitstaff about wine appreciation for years, and I have realized that new drinkers simply cannot get past the burning sensation in their noses.

This exercise can help new drinkers minimize alcohol burn and actually taste what they are drinking. It acclimates the nose to the rising alcohol vapors. Then the brain can process the flavor of the wine instead of the sting of the alcohol.

1. Place the wine in your mouth for ten seconds without swallowing. Breathe through your nose (or your mouth if you can manage it).
2. Swallow the wine, then immediately sip and swallow a little more wine.
3. Now take a breath of fresh air. You will notice the details that make that wine unique.

Beginning wine drinkers can also start with sweet wines or low-alcohol wines. It can take years to get used to alcohol, but don't get discouraged. Wine appreciation is a journey, not a destination.

Developing Your Palate

Everyone's palate is different. For instance, people who love sweets don't usually like bitter or tannic wines. My mother has a big sweet tooth, and a big red wine is never going to satisfy her. It is absolutely not her style. Smokers have less-sensitive taste buds, so they often go for bigger, more tannic wines. It takes a lot of character to surprise a smoker. So whether someone smokes sporadically or constantly, they are just more accustomed to richer flavors.

That being said, your palate changes as you sample more wines. Today you may not like cabernet sauvignon, but if you keep trying new wines, one day you probably will. The same goes for every other grape variety. I had a friend who bought five cases of his favorite wine to keep for years. After one year he had four cases left, and he didn't like the wine nearly as much. He was appreciating other new wines instead. To avoid this situation, if you really like a particular wine, start with a case of six or twelve bottles and see how it goes.

Now grab your wine journal, because it's time to develop your palate.

Try Lots of Wines

So you know what you like. Isn't that enough? In a word, yes! But how do you find out what you like when there are thousands of different types of wine and over three hundred thousand different wine labels in the world? Well, practice makes perfect. Try as many as you can, and keep track of them as you go. I recommend keeping a wine journal to document what wines you like and dislike. This way you can recall which grape varieties, regions, and vintages spark your fancy, along with those that don't.

Shun Peer Pressure

The most important rule of wine appreciation is to drink what you like. Do not believe that you must like a wine because it has been highly rated by a magazine or because your friend's boss says it is the best wine ever. Just as no two wines are exactly the same, no two people (and no two tongues) are the same.

This reminds me of the durian, a fruit commonly found in Southeast Asia. It is incredibly pungent even while in its husk. In Singapore, taking durian onto public transportation, including taxis, is illegal because of its smell. Some describe the aroma as a sweet fragrance; others say it smells like rotten onions or raw sewage. And I haven't even begun to describe the taste! We all have different senses of smell and taste, so wine ratings and the opinions of others should be considered guidelines, not facts.

Only Buy What You Can Afford

The second most important rule of selecting a wine is to buy only what you can afford. If you are new to drinking wine, there is no reason to jump right into the more expensive wines. It just isn't worth the extra cash. Save your money for another bottle of a different grape variety or region.

After you drink wine for a few years, your palate becomes more sophisticated, and you pinpoint your favorite grape varieties or styles. At this point, you can begin to pay more for wine. One can only hope that your budget for such indulgences increases along with your acumen. Ultimately, you will be left with a choice: drink less wine and more of the good stuff, or just keep drinking what suits your needs.

If I'm in the United States, I rarely spend less than twenty dollars a bottle. Are there good wines available for less than that? Yes! But I have gotten picky and would rather spend twenty dollars on a wine I know I will like than ten dollars on something I don't know. Sometimes, though, I go through experimental phases and buy fifteen-dollar bottles I haven't tried. New regions and unknown grape varieties occasionally appear, and one may just be a gem. I have had a couple of wines from Georgia and Russia that impressed me (along with a few that I could not finish).

Finding More Wines You Like

Trying to choose a bottle of wine can be overwhelming. Where in the world did the wine come from? Are you buying at a store, a winery, online? Are you buying the wine as a gift, for a dinner party, for a quiet night at home? All of this affects your choice. Luckily, you have some helpful resources that can help you pick.

Wine Apps

There are many wine apps out there that let you browse different wines and interact with communities of wine lovers. You can see what other people are drinking and "follow" those who share your tastes in wine. A wine app is also a great way to keep a personal wine journal, since you probably have your smartphone with you most of the time. This can help you select wines at a wine shop or a restaurant. One of the better wine apps is Vivino; the label scanner is quite accurate, and the community is lively.

Wine Fairs

At wine fairs, newbies and veterans alike can try lots of wine at an affordable price. Wine fairs are quite trendy and are popping up all over the place. Just remember to spit the wine out when attending the fairs (most people can't tell the difference between wines after the fifth tasting). Take your time, start with white wines, and keep your palate cleansed with water and simple foods.

Wineries

Wineries—and their tasting rooms—are getting more and more common. Winery staff are often happy to teach you a thing or two about wine as they pour you tastings. Tell the experts behind the counter what you like so they can suggest appropriate wines. Some places provide complimentary tastings with a purchase; others offer free tastings regardless of whether or not you make a purchase.

Raise Your Glass

The most important rule about drinking wine is to drink what you like. But it's difficult to know what you like if you always buy the same wines or your nose stings every time you take a sip. Even if you are open to trying new things, it may be tempting to grab the first bottle you see rather than sift through countless wines. I'll help you navigate this red-and-white sea in the next chapter.

CHAPTER 6

Where to Buy Wine

When you walk into a bar, there are generally a few local beers and a few imported beers on the menu. When it comes to wine, though, anywhere from ten to one hundred wines is normal. The restaurant next door may have a completely different and equally large list. The wine shop across the street stocks five hundred more wines you have never heard of, and the supermarket where you buy a bottle or two a month has another five hundred wines. No wonder people find choosing wine so confusing!

Who decides which wines are available, and what do they base their selections on? Where is the best place to buy wine, anyway? How can anyone make any sense of all this? If you follow a few simple rules, choosing wine will no longer feel like such a daunting task.

The Journey to the Consumer

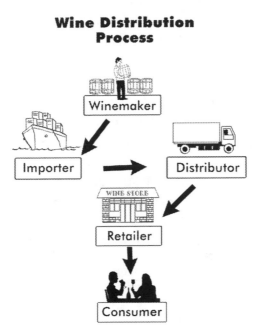

Wine Distribution Process

I refer to all the decision makers along the wine distribution and retail process as the gatekeepers. Once a wine is made, an importer can choose to represent the wine. After an importer decides which wines to represent, it offers portions of its portfolio to distributors. Those distributors may offer portions of their portfolios to subdistributors. Then the distributors and subdistributors show their offerings to hotels, restaurants, and wine shops. Only once the gatekeepers have made all their decisions do you get to choose your wine.

By the time you order your wine at a restaurant or hotel, the wine probably has been tasted a few times by the importer, a couple of times by the distributor, and at least once by someone in the restaurant. If you are buying it in a store, the importer, distributer, and stocking personnel have sampled it. Each of those people has his or her own preferences and beliefs that affect what the customer gets to drink.

Costco is a great example of this. This US chain of stores is very large, and each store is huge as well. Many foreigners can't believe their eyes when they first enter a Costco, which sells just about everything: luggage, clothes, salmon, car parts, shampoo, and, of course, wine. In fact, Costco is one of the largest wine buyers in the United States.

When Costco's head wine buyer, an experienced sommelier, left for another job, he was replaced by the head of the automotive and electronics department. This made Annette Alvarez-Peters, who didn't know much about wine, one of the most powerful wine buyers in the world. She was offered a very nice, all-expenses-paid trip to visit the top wineries in France to learn about wines. What a great experience that must have been! She was tasting the most highly regarded wines in the world straight from the barrel.

A US news station interviewed Alvarez-Peters after she had tasted a few wines. The reporter asked her what she thought about the experience and the wines. Her response was that she was having a lovely time, but as a businessperson sourcing products for her company, she felt that wine was "just a beverage."

"Is it more special than clothing?" she asked the reporter. "Is it more special than televisions? I don't think so."

"Certainly it's different than toilet paper, or different than tin foil," said the reporter.

"Why?" asked Alvarez-Peters.

"Because it's personal."

"People can look at it that way," said Alvarez-Peters. "But at the end of the day, it's a beverage!"[16]

Of course, she is correct. Wine is a beverage. But you can imagine the uproar in the wine world when this hit the press. The point is that every wine buyer has something to contribute to the selection process, including the head wine buyer at Costco, who thinks that wine is as special as toilet paper.

Other wine buyers have finicky requirements for their wines. I remember when I first starting traveling around the United States selling PengWine. I went into a popular neighborhood restaurant in Texas, and the owner asked me if my wines were available in the local supermarket.

"No," I said with some pride.

He smiled. "Good. I do not want the same wines on my wine list as those in the local supermarket," he explained. "That way no one questions the pricing!"

An hour later I went to another restaurant in the same neighborhood. When the owner asked if my wines were available in the local supermarket, I confidently told him that they were not.

This time, the owner shook his head. "That's too bad," he said. "I only serve wine that the local consumers already know—so they feel comfortable."

I was stumped, and now I was nervous about going to the next restaurant. There is no magic sales code in this industry; everyone is looking for something different.

As soon as a wine makes it onto a menu, its price swells. A wine that is fifteen dollars down the street is seventy-five dollars on a wine list. If you want a nice bottle of wine with dinner, you are forced to pay whatever the restaurant charges. The more expensive the restaurant, the higher the markup on the average bottle. And when you are at that remote island resort, you can expect to empty your bank account for something you would never drink at home.

The Mysteries of Wine Pricing

There are enough experts, sommeliers, wine buyers, distributors, and wine critics to ensure that fair wine prices are generally upheld. But even when prices are just, many people do not understand why wines are priced the way they are. While prices are largely dependent on the way the wine is made (slow wines cost more than fast wines) and on terroir (established wine regions reap higher prices), there are a few other elements that matter.

Your Geographic Location

Did you know that the most expensive state in the United States to buy Californian wine is California? And did you know that most wines are more expensive when you buy them at the winery, unless you are a member of their club? Conversely, anyone who has been to France, Italy, or Spain knows that great local wines are cheap—cheaper than bottled water. Each wine region does things differently. Chile, for instance, exports up to 97 percent of its wine. Argentina produces four times the amount of wine as Chile, yet Chile still exports twice as much wine as Argentina. This just means that Argentinians drink more of their wine. In most countries, the locals make sure the tastiest wines with the best prices stay at home.

What does this mean for you? Figure out what the best deals in your area are, and buy those locally. The best deals may be wines from your region or may be something completely different. If you want to try something that is overpriced in your area, consider ordering it online (I will examine online wine buying more in a moment).

Vintage

One of the most influential factors on wine pricing is vintage. Wines from vintage years cost more. Also, the older the vintage of a slow wine, the higher the price tag because of the storage time and investment.

If you are new to wines, don't worry about purchasing expensive vintage slow wines just yet. But if you are ready for vintages and don't want to be duped, do your research before buying. I know of a Chinese wine that has been made for over seven years, yet according to the bottles, they were all produced in 2008. Every vintage is the same year, according to the bottles. I suspect this is because the number eight is very auspicious in China.

Awards

As I mentioned, awards and high scores from wine critics boost wine prices. But trust me—this extra income does not usually go to the producers; it just helps producers to get importers and distributors. The higher profits go to the middlemen, even though the producer created the award-winning wine.

Where to Buy

After all my rants and raves about buying wine, you may well be wondering where you should buy wine in the first place. The truth is, I usually drink my own wine! In the industry, we also trade wines whenever possible, so I get a lot of wine that way. But I do have some advice for wine shoppers too. After all, I used to be one.

Stores

The first thing a wine salesperson asks is always simple: "How much do you want to spend?" This is because just about every type of wine exists at multiple price points. If you want a light red wine, you can get one for twenty dollars or for one hundred dollars. If you like sweet white wines, then yep, you guessed it: that wine is available for twenty dollars and one hundred dollars too. Just remember to stick to your budget even when buying gifts. You may be tempted to buy a fifty-dollar bottle for your boss, even though your budget is thirty dollars. After all, your boss is worth it, right? Funny how we often spend more on others than we spend on ourselves.

Not sure what to get? Many wine shops have a few sample bottles of wines open. If the bottles are not on the counter, ask the shopkeeper what's behind the counter. Every shop has something open in the back.

I think the best question to ask the shopkeeper is "What would you drink?" This guarantees that the salesperson won't simply sell you overstocked wines. That said, if the salesperson is in his or her early twenties and you are in your forties, there is a strong likelihood that you don't like the same wines. In that situation, you may want to ask what the salesperson's mom likes to drink!

Online

It took much longer for online wine sales to catch on than the industry first predicted, but it eventually happened. At first, sales were slow because consumers were afraid to use credit card information for online purchases. The next deterrent was the high cost of shipping; there are many laws and regulations that make the process complicated and pricey. These are still large hindrances for online wine orders, especially in the United States. Even so, the Internet has transformed wine sales all over the world.

When e-commerce first began, everyone with a product got excited and created a website. It turned out that people used the Internet to do product research and compare prices but still went to brick-and-mortar stores to purchase their items. After all, why would people buy a wine online if they have no idea what it tastes like? I will be very happy if we can taste wines over the Internet someday (then again, I might never leave my computer).

There are many sites that offer wine deals—everything from mixed cases to 50 percent off bin ends. However, deals may not be as good as they seem: most wines are marked up 15 percent before they are offered to you at a 30 percent discount. Wine-Searcher.com is a good website for tracking the value of a bottle of wine, but even then you may find a crazy range of pricing. I once saw a bottle of PengWine listed for over $47,000! For that price, I would be willing to sell more than a few bottles from my private collection.

Wine Clubs

Online wine sales are increasing rapidly year after year, and it's not only because consumers are more comfortable with buying wine online. Even Wine.com, with its memorable name, filed for bankruptcy a few times before finally turning a profit. Online wine sales are taking off now because of online wine clubs. These clubs have learned that variety packs of wine make it easier for people to find new favorites. That, combined with lower shipping costs, is the perfect formula for enticing consumers.

Wine clubs offer a great and easy way to try lots of wines. The clubs do all the research and taste testing for you. Quite often they supply tasting notes and detailed information about the wines' producers as well. Larger wine clubs also have the power of bulk shipping, which reduces costs for everyone.

Buying Direct

The beauty of buying wine directly from the producer (or from an appointed representative in your country) is that your purchase price goes directly to the winemaker. Most small winemakers struggle financially; good wine is not cheap to make, and small ventures must compete with huge wineries that have large productions and massive distribution channels. Therefore, small winemakers are very appreciative when people buy directly.

Wine Investments

Believe it or not, some wine investments have outperformed many stocks for decades. As long as there are people willing to pay exorbitant prices for the status that comes with drinking fine wine, there is no end in sight. However, unless you are a big player, I would only recommend investing in wines that you actually intend to drink.

If you are looking to resell wines yourself, you are not investing wisely. There is an entire wine investment industry, and I leave wine investing to brokers the same way I leave the stock market to professional investors. It's not always easy to find a wine buyer, and if you can't prove that the wine is authentic or that it has been stored perfectly, it is nearly impossible to make a profit.

Counterfeit wines are yet another concern. European wines are particularly popular in China, and counterfeiters there tend to focus on French wine. Take 1982 Lafite, a wine worth nearly $4,000 today. I've heard that there are more cases of 1982 Lafite in China than were actually produced by the vineyard. Fake Lafite isn't the only concern; labels capitalizing on the name recognition of established brands have emerged on the market, including Chatelet Lafite (a play on the Lafite trademark).

I have lived in Chile, the United States, and Australia. I bought wines that I enjoyed and put a few aside as an investment in my future enjoyment of wine. Basically, if you buy it, plan to drink it!

Buy Wisely

Unless you have had a wine before, you have absolutely no idea what is in the bottle. Let's face it: no matter where you buy a wine, ultimately you just want to like it. And if you are giving it as a gift, you hope that the recipient likes it too. The best thing you can do is to keep recording wines in your wine notebook. That way, you will make better and more-informed decisions every time you buy a new bottle of wine.

CHAPTER 7

Wine Pairing from a Chef's Point of View

You may know some rules about pairing wine with food. Forget all of them. There are no concrete guidelines as to which wines accompany specific foods. Finding the right wine to pair with a meal is much like finding the right wines to line your cupboard. It all depends on what you like and what your taste buds tell you complements the dish.

Trapped by Convention

The old belief that red meat should be paired with red wine and that seafood must be paired with white wine does not always apply. I will never forget the time I was challenged on this very issue at the launch of PengWine's premium wine, the Emperor. The event was sold out, and since it was held at one of the most exclusive private clubs in the world, many experienced wine drinkers were slated to attend. A week prior to the event, the executive chef and I did a complete taste test of the five-course dinner and paired a different PengWine wine with each course. One of the courses was seared salmon with a red wine sauce made with the PengWine Rockhopper. Since the wine was already in the sauce, we decided to pair the Rockhopper with the dish.

On the day of the event, I had a great time talking with all the guests. Between each course, I got up in front of the whole gathering and explained the wine pairing for the next dish. Everyone seemed to be having a great time.

As everyone tucked into the penultimate course, I approached a table and asked how everything tasted.

"Are you a fucking idiot?"

I could not believe my own ears. "I'm sorry; what are you referring to?" I asked the irate man.

"Everyone knows you don't serve a red wine with fish," said the man. He was truly offended, and he didn't hesitate to continue to let me know it.

I took the opportunity to try to educate the guest. I explained that, since the sauce was the dominant flavor in the dish, it was important to pair the wine to the sauce. I explained that because the sauce was made with the same exact wine that was paired with the dish, there was an even higher level of harmony.

"Do you feel that the wine does not go with the dish?" I asked him finally.

"I refuse to even try the wine with the dish," he said. "It is an insult to me to even try a red wine with a fish." He demanded a white wine and added a few more myopic words. I was left with no choice but to smile, thank him for coming, and walk away. The guest did eat the fish—with a glass of white wine, of course.

This left me thinking about where people get their information about wine. I am not trying to change what people like about wine. But for heaven's sake, try to be open-minded about pairing food with what is, after all, just fermented grape juice. Would that man insist that only Coca-Cola goes with pizza? Probably not.

Learning to Pair Wines

When pairing a specific dish with a wine, there are lots of things to consider. What is in the dish? What country is the recipe from? How was the wine made? By thinking about the many factors the influence food and wine, you can find a wonderful match for any meal.

Protein Power

Most often there is a main ingredient to a dish, and usually this is a protein. Sometimes this is meat, such as beef, lamb, duck, or chicken. At other times, it may be fish or other seafood. Still other time there may be a vegetarian protein or no main protein at all.

Why am I emphasizing proteins so much? Many of them have unique flavors, and wines have been categorized to match specific protein flavors. For example, lamb is distinctively stronger in flavor than beef, and whitefish is milder than salmon. However, once other ingredients, such as herbs, spices, and sauces, and even cooking methods are applied, the intensity of the dish changes completely, and the pairing of wine should be reconsidered. With pasta and vegetarian dishes, it's about the full impact of the ingredients.

Tastes Matter

Most dishes are served with sides that complement not just the main ingredient but also the entire dish. Wine should be paired with food in the same way. The most important thing to evaluate is the intensity of the dish. Is it mild, bold, spicy, complex? Also focus on the dominant flavor of the food. What flavors really stand out? Perhaps the main flavor is an herb, such as rosemary or basil. Maybe it's garlic or onion. It could even be acid, such as vinegar or lemon juice. Then again, it may be a spicy flavor, such as peppers. In the case of the seared salmon with the red wine sauce, the red wine sauce dominated the flavor of the salmon, and the red wine from which the sauce was derived was the natural pairing.

I have summarized some categories of flavors and the grape varieties most suited to pair with them at the back of this book. However, please don't use this as the last word on your wine pairings. Through your own trial and error, you will find that some wines don't pair well with certain cuisines and others pair wonderfully. I love spicy food with a riesling from Germany, which may have a very slight sweetness to it. I even enjoy riesling with salty french fries. I like a nice cabernet sauvignon with a good steak, and I have even had a chardonnay or two that go well with steak.

How Was It Made?

It helps to understand how a wine was made when pairing it with food. For example, the chardonnays that I enjoy with grilled steak are usually ones that were fermented in oak barrels. These chardonnays have a smoky, oaky profile that complements the BBQ. All I have to do is ignore my oak allergy and enjoy!

It's a Small World

Wines can also be paired with food according to where the cuisines originate. Generally, Mediterranean cuisines are the easiest to match. Lebanese, Greek, Italian, French, and Spanish cuisines lend themselves to a variety of wines since most wines are produced in Mediterranean climates. Tropical cuisines are trickier to pair with wine since countries like Thailand, Mexico, Cuba, Indonesia, and Singapore all have very different styles of cuisine.

Buying Wine for a Hosted Event

If you are attending an event and want to take a bottle or two of wine along, be sure to take something appropriate. If you are going to a cocktail or dinner party, you may wish to ask what is on the menu or how many people will attend. A fine twenty-year-old bottle of your favorite wine is likely not the right choice for a casual thirty-person gathering, for example.

If a nice bottle is appropriate for the event, by all means take one. But have you ever taken a good wine to a friend's house only to have the friend place it on the back counter and offer you a glass of whatever was on sale at the supermarket? And then your friend opens three more bottles of the same wine? Who knows if that nice bottle you brought will ever be truly enjoyed?

To avoid this situation, consider telling the host that you are especially looking forward to sharing that bottle with them and that you picked it out just for that evening. It not only flatters the host but also ensures that you get to savor at least a glass of decent wine.

Receiving Wine at a Hosted Event

What should you do when someone brings a bottle of wine to your house for a dinner or a party? If you are hosting an event for fellow wine lovers, everyone usually brings something to share and discuss. This is a great way to taste everyone's favorite wines.

On the flip side, let's say you are hosting a dinner. You have already opened the wines you've chosen to pair with the meal, and they have been breathing nicely for hours. Then a friend brings a bottle and tells you that he or she picked it just for the occasion. You have two options. You could politely mention that you already have wines picked out for the dinner and offer to wait to open the bottle until the next time that person comes over. Or, of course, you could open the bottle later if there is an appropriate time during the evening. There's nothing wrong with a little extra wine, right?

If you think your guest has brought you a fine wine and you are not sure if you should open it or save it, you can always ask. If it's a wine that you should save for a while, then I suggest you write a little note on the bottle specifying who gave it to you and when you received it. Even if you open the wine two years later, it's always nice to think of that person as you drink the wine. Perhaps it's the perfect reason to reach out and thank them again. Share the love when you share the wine.

Eat, Drink, and Be Merry

Pairing wine with food does not have to be an ordeal. Use the list in the back of this book as a guide, but don't forget to experiment and follow your instincts. You may well find that a red wine pairs well with a spicy shrimp dish or that an oaked white wine tastes great with a cut of venison. Don't be afraid to break all the rules—you might be pleasantly surprised.

PART III

DRINKING WINE

CHAPTER 8

The Wine Survival Kit

There's a gadget for everything nowadays. You can get a self-sanitizing toothbrush, an automatic vacuum cleaner, or even a multi-temperature wine fridge. Wine has become so trendy that wine products are getting a little ridiculous. Wine lovers can now get instant chillers, automatic cork pullers, and fancy picnic baskets with slots for wine bottles. The question is, which gadgets are worth your money and which ones should be left on the shelf?

Wineglasses

I am often asked about the importance of the right wineglass. While the shape and size of a wineglass matter, they don't make as much of a difference as some people think. Scientists once believed that only certain parts of the tongue could sense certain flavors; you may have heard that your tongue tastes sweetness at the front and bitterness at its sides, for instance. The glass companies even claimed that their glasses made wine land on the perfect parts of the tongue to maximize enjoyment and evaluation. However, it has now been proven that all parts of your tongue can equally sense all tastes, so glassmakers have to think of another marketing strategy.

While wineglasses may not be designed based on tongue anatomy anymore, there are certain features that influence your wine-drinking experience. A glass needs enough surface area to allow the drinker to properly evaluate the wine. However, if the wineglass is too big, the aromas won't concentrate at the top of the glass. Regardless of the size, the shape of the wineglass affects the smell and therefore the taste of the wine; certain companies claim that their glasses have the perfect shape for each style of wine.

The same wine companies that instructed drinkers to only hold the stem of the wineglass (so as not to leave fingerprints or warm the wine) also invented the stemless wineglass. The stemless wineglass has its advantages: it easily fits into dishwashers and cabinets, for one. However, I prefer stemmed glasses for the very benefits previously mentioned.

Decanters and Aerators

I will discuss the purpose and methods of decanting and aerating in the next chapter. For now, just know that decanters should have wider bases than a wine bottle, since pouring the wine from the bottle into the decanter is supposed to add surface area to the wine. Pouring wine into a narrow cylinder does not do much good. The most traditional decanter is called a duck because it is literally shaped like—you guessed it—a duck.

Decanters come in many shapes and sizes, but all of them should be made of glass. Wine may stain plastic and even pick up some plastic flavor, and clear glass displays the color of the wine. An aerator, which is typically small and portable, expedites the process of decanting by forcing oxygen into the wine.

Wine Openers

Waiter's friend corkscrew

A waiter's-friend corkscrew is the most traditional wine opener. It has a knife on one end to cut the foil and has either a single or a double hinge. I prefer the double hinge style. It also has a corkscrew (auger).

Lever corkscrews are handy as well; the wide bottom can replace a cork in a pinch.

Lever corkscrew

Ah-so two-prong cork puller

The Ah-So two-prong cork puller is another favorite. It looks like a key and does not have a corkscrew at all. You simply slide the two prongs down between the cork and the bottle and then twist while pulling up to remove the cork. I have never broken a cork using an Ah-So.

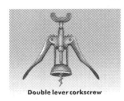

Le Creuset wine opener

Le Creuset, a kitchenware company, makes a great table wine opener. It looks like a double-lever corkscrew, but it does not have levers at all. Instead, it has two notches that hold it in place while you screw the corkscrew into the cork. As you turn the corkscrew, because the notches hold the device in place, the cork is pulled straight up into the corkscrew instead of the corkscrew screwing down into the cork.

You should stay away from the double-lever corkscrew, which looks like a little person with a bottle cap remover for a head. Conceptually they are a good idea, but they do not work very well in practice. Often they do not pull the cork straight up, so they break a lot of corks. They have broken many bottles as well. They are very common, and people look for them, but I always cringe when somebody hands me one.

Double lever corkscrew

Electric wine openers are gaining popularity, but I do not like them, especially for opening older wines. The electric contraption hides the cork, so you can't tell if the cork is starting to break. If you use a handheld cork puller, you can tell if the cork is breaking and adjust your technique accordingly.

Wine Pourers and Drip Controllers

Drip stop PVC disc

When pouring a red wine, I always get at least one drip down the label. And of course, spilled red wine can ruin furniture and clothing. In the United States, a company called DropStop has trademarked and patented a product that solves this issue. DropStop pour disks are circular metallic PVC disks that roll up and fit into the mouth of the bottle, forming a spout. They stop dripping and help control pouring. A wine collar or drip-stop collar (a little cylinder that goes around the top of the bottle) helps with dripping as well.

Stoppers

A wine stopper is no longer just a plug. Today, you can get everything from air removal pumps to wine preservation systems. If I open a bottle of wine, I don't need a stopper, because the wine will be gone in a few hours. If you tend to leave wines open for a few days, I think wine preservation systems are the best choice. They replace the air in the top of the wine bottle with inert gas, eliminating oxidation and helping the wine stay fresh.

Wine Dispensers

A wine dispenser works like an automatic soda fountain. A big one holds four or five bottles at a time and connects to an inert gas system. These gadgets are expensive—they start at about $1,000 apiece—but they are definitely nice to have.

If you can't afford your own wine dispenser, you can go out and try one. There are many new restaurants and wine bars that have dozens of wines in dispensers. You put your credit card in the machine and pick whichever wine you want, and the machine fills your glass for you. This makes it possible to try lots of wines without committing to purchasing a bottle.

Wine Fridges

Wine fridges have their place. They keep wine correctly stored for a long time, but they are not usually necessary. Some people tell me, "Oh, I don't buy a lot of wine, because I don't have a wine fridge." Believe it or not, in the 1800s, they did not have wine fridges either. Wine drinkers got along very well without them for thousands of years, and so can you.

Nose-Training Kits

Aroma-training kits contain lots of scents in tiny bottles. Using these scents, you can train yourself to detect various smells more accurately. What does this have to do with wine? By strengthening your nose, you can teach yourself to recognize these smells in other situations, such as in wines. So if you have no idea how some people can smell pine or cranberries or pineapple in a wine, one of these kits may do you a lot of good.

What to Put in Your Wine Survival Kit

Now that you know what's out there, it's time to decide what you should actually invest in. Most new wine drinkers don't need a lot of equipment. For example, I think a decanter is unnecessary for new wine drinkers because they drink a lot of younger wines that don't need decanting. However, a few basic supplies can go a long way toward bettering your wine journey.

Decent Glasses

Nice glasses do count for something. The concentration of aromas absolutely changes with the shape of the glass, and your nose reacts before your tongue even touches the wine. I would not worry too much about the shape of the glass until you understand the common traits of a few grape varieties; instead, focus on size. Find a medium-size glass for white wines and a slightly larger glass for red wines. Then again, if you end up in a situation where all you have is a red Solo cup, don't worry about it.

Wine Opener

Every wine drinker needs a wine opener. Besides double-lever corkscrews and electric wine openers, any of the wine openers I mentioned earlier are fine. The Le Creuset table wine opener is probably the easiest to use. Do not get lured in by the fancy electric wine openers; they just aren't worth the hype.

Other Equipment

A wine fridge may be overkill, but an insulator, a canister, or an ice bucket comes in handy. Such a product lets you keep chilled wine on the table during or after a meal.

If you don't have DropStop pour disks or a wine collar (or even if you do), keep a towel nearby. A wine coaster or another surface that you consistently put the bottle down on is a good idea. If you are a red wine drinker, you should always have a bottle of Wine Away red wine stain remover. It has saved many of my white shirts.

I also recommend label removers and a notebook. Everyone thinks that they will remember which wines they have had, but when they walk into a wine shop and see hundreds of bottles, their minds go blank. Label removers let you cleanly remove labels from bottles and stick them in your notebook. With a notebook full of labels, you can keep track of what you have had, what you like, and what you do not like. Your smartphone works well for this too.

Wine-Equipment Shopping List

- medium white wineglasses
- large red wineglasses
- Le Creuset table wine opener
- ice bucket
- DropStop pour disks

- Wine Away red wine stain remover
- label removers and a notebook (or wine journal app)

Wine Over Matter

In the end, a roomful of swanky wine gadgets does not make you a more informed wine drinker. As long as you have a few essentials and keep trying and tracking wines, your palate will develop nicely. You don't need a state-of-the-art home wine dispenser and several sets of crystal glasses. So gather your wine necessities, fill your appropriately sized glass, and read on.

CHAPTER 9

At Your Service

At this point, you know a few things about wine. You know how it is made, what is in it, and how it is labeled. You know the difference between merlot and chardonnay, and hopefully you know which one you prefer. You have the equipment you need to properly enjoy wine (and you know what you definitely don't need). Congratulations for coming this far! Now that you know all this, it's time to learn how to store and serve this irresistible elixir.

Storing Wine

Once you have purchased some delicious wines, you need to keep them somewhere (unless you plan on drinking them immediately). Whatever you do, don't throw them on top of your refrigerator! One of the worst places to store wine, and sadly one of the most common, is the top of the fridge. There is a reason why wine is traditionally kept in dark, cool, and quiet wine cellars: temperature changes, vibrations, and sunlight harm wine. The back of the refrigerator creates a lot of heat, and that heat travels right up to the top of the refrigerator (you don't notice it, because you never sit on top of the refrigerator, but it gets pretty warm up there). The refrigerator is also always vibrating, and vibration changes the chemical aging process of a wine and causes it to break down.

Have you ever wondered why wine usually comes in green bottles? It is to keep UV rays away. UV rays break down most foods; that is why even milk is packaged in translucent or opaque containers more often than clear ones. Wines that come in clear bottles are generally standard or fast wines that should be consumed promptly.

If you aren't fortunate enough to have space for a wine cellar, store your wine in an internal closet with little temperature variation. And don't just place the bottles upright on the closet floor. Wine corks expand in the bottle when they moisten; if the bottle stays upright, no wine is in contact with the cork, and so the cork dries up and shrinks, letting oxygen into the bottle. Therefore, always store wine bottles horizontally.

Opening Wine

As long as you have a decent wine opener, opening wine is a fairly simple process. If there is foil sealing off the cork, you can use a small knife or your fingers to remove it prior to opening the bottle. Then simply insert the corkscrew or pointy portion of the wine opener into the cork, then either pull or use the lever to open the bottle. However, if you've ever forgotten your cork puller or broken a cork, you know that some situations necessitate some creative maneuvering.

Opening Wine without a Cork Puller

Two nights ago, I was at a golf course at ten o'clock at night with some friends and an unopened bottle of wine. None of us had cork pullers. What did we do? There are lots of YouTube videos showing crazy ways to remove wine corks, such as putting the bottle in your shoe and slamming it against a wall. Sounds like a great way to break some glass and spill wine everywhere!

Here's my advice: just push the cork very gently into the bottle. Keep a towel over the top of whatever you are using to push the cork in, as the wine will likely splash a bit. Or, if you can, choose a bottle with a screw top for the most flexibility.

What If the Cork Breaks?

If the cork breaks, it doesn't necessarily mean that the wine is bad; it could be the wine puller (especially if you are using a bad lever cork puller). If the cork crumbles, simply exercise extra scrutiny when tasting the wine (you will learn how to identify a faulty wine in the next chapter). If the wine tastes okay, pour the liquid through a clean paper coffee filter or cheesecloth to get rid of any crumbled cork pieces.

Let It Breathe

Oxygen can be a wine's best friend or its worst enemy. During the wine creation process, as I already mentioned, wine is exposed to oxygen. The process of decanting purposefully exposes wine to oxygen right after a bottle is opened. During storage, conversely, oxygen should be kept away. Even once it is opened, too much decanting can kill a wine. Here is everything you need to know about the love-hate relationship between oxygen and wine.

Decanting and Oxidation

Have you ever left pieces of avocado or apple out on the counter? What happened? They probably turned brown and started to taste different. This happens to wine too, and it's called oxidation. Exposure to oxygen after fermentation causes a wine to oxidize, changing its chemical composition and thus its flavor.

Like a piece of fruit left out too long, an oxidized wine darkens. It begins to smell bad; any fruity notes in the original scent of a red wine disappear, and white wines might start smelling like sherry or apple cider. Think of the way wine tastes when it is left open for five days—most people notice a funky flavor when a wine has been left open for that long.[17] While avocados and apples oxidize quickly, wine takes a while to oxidize (especially red wines, which oxidize over several days).

Decanting a wine, on the other hand, is the process of adding oxygen to a wine soon before drinking it. Remember that wine is alive. Imagine that you have been stuffed inside a bottle for many years, and finally, one day, you are set free. What is the first thing you want to do? Take a big deep breath and stretch. That's exactly what a wine wants to do too.

You would never decant a fruit or vegetable, but decanting has a wonderful effect on many wines. It reduces certain compounds in the wine, including sulfides, sulfites, and ethanol. This allows more-desirable flavors of the wine to shine through.

Micro-oxygenation

Micro-oxygenation is a relatively new concept. It was invented in the early 1990s and became extremely popular, in part, thanks to French oenologist Michel Rolland. Rolland was a prominent figure in the 2004 documentary *Mondovino* (which means "worldwine" in Italian). He wasn't the inventor of micro-oxygenation, but he told winemakers that it was the solution for everything. Wine too acidic? Micro-oxygenate. Too tannic? Micro-oxygenate. Got stuck at fermentation? Micro-oxygenate! Rolland has since denied advocating the technique, but the damage has been done.[18]

When wine is barrel aging, chemical changes soften and mellow it. When the wine is bottled, it should continue to mature until it is poured and allowed to breathe. Aging changes everything about wine: colors, aroma, mouth feel, and flavors. Micro-oxygenation mimics this aging process in a fraction of the time (and a fraction of the cost). During micro-oxygenation, a ceramic ball filled with oxygen is dropped into a tank of wine. The oxygen then bubbles through the wine, mimicking the aging process.

Pumping oxygen into wine is very cheap, so lots of wineries do it. The catch is that once you micro-oxygenate a wine, you increase the risk of spoiling it. Think back to standard and fast wines, for which the vintage is more or less an expiration date. Wineries micro-oxygenate these wines to make them ready to drink as soon as the bottles are opened. If you decant such a wine, you are actually double decanting it, and it may go bad. This is why fast wines don't last for more than a day after they are opened. The wines were already oxidizing in the bottle, and opening the bottle ruins the wine within a few hours. A well-made red wine that has not been micro-oxygenated, on the other hand, can still taste great after five days of sitting on the counter.

There is no way to tell whether or not a wine has been micro-oxygenated, but it's likely that more than half of all wine produced today is micro-oxygenated (thanks, Michel Rolland).

Oxidation vs. Micro-oxygenation

I know it's confusing, but remember that oxidation and micro-oxygenation are two different things.

> **oxidation**: The chemical change triggered by oxygen that causes wine to spoil. This is why wine goes bad after you open the bottle.

> **micro-oxygenation**: Injecting wine with oxygen during the production process.

How to Decant

To decant a wine that has not been micro-oxygenated, simply pour it into a vessel larger than the wine bottle. Many people think that decanting is only for red wines, but it can make some white wines more enjoyable as well. I have even heard of people decanting sparkling wines, but I don't recommend that, because it can decrease carbonation.

Before decanting a wine, taste it and decide whether it needs the extra step. Even if I know I want to decant a wine, I like to sample it and take note of the aromas and sensations. This allows me to gauge the effect of the decanting process.

How Long to Decant

How long should you decant a wine? It ranges. Some wines can take hours and hours to finally show their true potential. Some PengWine wines can breathe for days and just keep getting better. That's not to say that these wines are not enjoyable as soon as the cork is pulled; it's just that they get better as they breathe.

Do keep one rule in mind: opening a wine bottle, pouring the wine into the decanter, and then immediately filling a few glasses does not do anything. If you are planning on having wine at home, decant it for at least an hour beforehand. For red wines, I recommend one to two hours; for white wines, I recommend an hour. Keeping wines cool during decanting can be tricky, but you can decant in the fridge if you need to (if, of course, there is room in the fridge).

Decanting Older Wines

To properly decant a wine that is over five years old, ensure that the wine has been standing upright for at least a day. Wine produces sediment as it ages, and standing the bottle upright allows the sediment to sink. This reduces the risk of pouring gunk into the decanter and into your glass.

When the time comes to decant the wine, pour it slowly to avoid disrupting the sediment. Traditionally, people place a candle under the neck of the bottle as they pour; this reveals when the sediment has reached the neck of the bottle, which is an indication that it is time to stop pouring. You could always use a flashlight if you have one available, but if you are in a well-lit room and you pour slowly enough, you should not need a candle or a flashlight.

Serving Temperature

In the United States, almost all drinks are served chilled. But outside of the United States, people don't really drink a lot of iced beverages. In fact, ice has only been accessible for about 150 years. In the 1800s man-made ice was nonexistent, and train cars refrigerated with natural ice were often used to transport goods. This made ice very valuable. Trains were built to carry ice from northern Canada to New York City. Workers filled the trains with huge blocks of ice, which melted down by 40 percent by the time they reached New York. Before all this happened, people relied on cellar temperatures to cool their wines. Drinking chilled white wine is a relatively recent phenomenon.

The general knowledge is that red wine should be served at room temperature and white wine should be served chilled. But as with all wine rules, this one is not necessarily true. Room temperature in France, where this rule originated, is 64 to 66 degrees Fahrenheit (18 to 19 degrees Celsius). I currently live in Singapore, where room temperature (with the air conditioner) is still about 75 degrees Fahrenheit (24 degrees Celsius). I tell people here to chill all wines, even red ones, because otherwise too much alcohol vapor lifts off the wine.

If the label of a bottle of red wine recommends room temperature, think about what your room temperature is. If it is over 66 degrees Fahrenheit (19 degrees Celsius), consider chilling your wine. Also, try chilling red wines if they are too harsh. I chill my red wine; sometimes I put a bottle of red wine in an ice bucket for five minutes or so, just to get it a little bit cooler than room temperature before serving. I always serve white wine at about 46 degrees Fahrenheit (8 degrees Celsius).

I think hot spiced wines are good, but I know a lot of people who turn their noses up at them. In keeping with my mantra, if you like wine at a certain temperature, then go for it.

Pour Your Wine and Drink It Too

Storing wine, decanting it, and serving it at the proper temperature are all important. But, of course, they are all means to one ultimate goal. Now we get to the really fun part: drinking wine.

CHAPTER 10

What's in Your Glass?
How to Evaluate Wine like a Pro

Have you ever seen someone swirling, sipping, and slurping wine at a party? You might have laughed at this once upon a time, but there is a good reason for this seemingly strange behavior. It becomes such a habit that I sometimes even swirl and smell my water before drinking it! And it all has to do with using as many senses as possible when trying wines.

The 5S Technique

I call the most popular wine-evaluation method the 5S technique. Wine judges, sommeliers, and winemakers all use this approach to consistently rank each new wine. Whether you are assessing wines or just relishing a glass at happy hour, this technique lets you fully appreciate what you are drinking.

The 5S Technique

1. See
2. Swirl
3. Smell
4. Sip
5. Savor

These five categories can be used to score wines in various ways. Some people make each category worth up to five points, for a total of twenty-five points possible per wine. Others feel that certain categories are more important than others and therefore assign them different values. For example, sight may have a scale of one to five, but sip may have a scale of one to ten.

If you choose to use a scoring system in your wine notebook, remember to be consistent. Use only two types of glasses (one for reds and one for whites) and stick to a single scoring system. Now let's start swirling, sipping, and slurping.

1. See

This category is about wine color and translucency. It's best to hold the glass at an angle above a plain white piece of paper when doing this. There are a few elements to look for: Is the wine dark and heavy or clear and light? Is there sediment in the glass? Is the wine the color you expect it to be? When you take note of these characteristics (and their relation to the grape), you set the foundation for the rest of the evaluation process. Experienced wine drinkers can tell the age of a wine by the color and hue around the edge of the liquid.

For safety reasons, make sure the wine is not bubbling unless it is supposed to be. It should not be cloudy either, unless it is an older wine and was not permitted to settle before pouring.

2. Swirl

One of the most common wine-snob habits is swirling a glass of wine all evening long. Some may think that such a person has a nervous twitch or just can't stay still. In fact, the wine snob is working. Swirling is a very important practice in wine appreciation because it incorporates more oxygen into the wine. Even if the wine has been decanted, swirling can help. Some wines open up quickly, while others take hours to show their true potential. If the wine has not been decanted, there is all the more reason to swirl it.

On top of incorporating oxygen, swirling wine creates a concentration of aromas at the top of the glass. If you swirl a wine and take a big sniff, the higher intensity makes subtle aromas more prominent. I like to cover the top of the glass with my hand as I swirl; this traps the smell and further maximizes the swirl effect.

Lastly, swirling a wine reveals color and creates "legs" on the sides of the glass. A wine's legs are the rivulets that drip down the inside of the glass. Many think that this says a lot about a wine, but in fact, the legs only divulge the viscosity (and thus the alcohol content) of the wine. There is no connection between legs and wine quality, though it may give you an idea of how the wine may feel in your mouth. Many beautiful long legs just indicate a lot of alcohol and a tall glass.

3. Smell

Some say that most of taste is smell. When it comes to wine, that is very true (assuming you have moved past the alcohol burn). However, scent is another area where experience comes into play. Each grape variety has its own unique aromas; for example, a sauvignon blanc may have lemongrass, green pepper, passion fruit, or asparagus notes. But these aromas vary and may sometimes not be detectable at all because of terroir, vintage, and the winemaker's style, not to mention your own evaluation skills. It's hard to be consistent, but practice sure helps!

Smelling the wine is also a way to check for faults. In the wine world, some smells indicate faults in the wine-making or aging process. One great example is the cork taint that I mentioned earlier. Typically corked wines are harmless, but they don't smell too appealing. Corked wines often smell like moldy newspaper, wet dog, or damp basement. Other faulty wines may smell like vinegar, wet cardboard, nail polish remover, or burnt toast. Each of these smells is caused by undesirable chemical changes in the wine and has a technical name, but we don't need to get into that here. Just remember that if the wine smells gross, you shouldn't put it in your mouth.

As with the entire process of wine evaluation, it's important to stay true to your opinions. Notice how quickly the mind agrees with what others say. If someone says they smell pineapple in a wine, you may quickly agree. But did pineapple really stand out to you before? If you are a new wine drinker, you have to be open to new ideas, but if you really don't smell pineapple, that is okay. Stick to your own senses.

4. Sip

Now for the moment of truth: the moment that you have been waiting for, the reason you have been seeing, smelling, and swirling. It's time to find out if the wine is all it's cracked up to be. You have prepared your senses for this moment, and the very second your tongue touches the wine, you are processing information.

First impressions are very important, but remember to take your time. Let the wine sit in your mouth for a few seconds. Move it around your mouth, and even breathe through your mouth around the wine. You may even wish to write a note or two before you swallow your first sip.

5. Savor

After you swallow, breathe through your mouth and pay attention to the finish. The moment after you swallow is referred to as the savor. This helps you judge the intensity of the wine. How does your mouth feel? Is the wine sweet? Sour? Is your tongue feeling dry? Perhaps you detect bitterness or feel the burn of alcohol down the back of your throat.

I recommend that you take at least two sips of a wine, following the same process as before. This allows for a more complete evaluation. I consider the first taste a palate cleanser and the second sip the moment of truth.

No matter what the sensations are, they are unique to you. Your notes should reflect your opinions and thoughts. When tasting a wine with other wine drinkers, I recommend adding other people's observations as side notes, regardless of whether you agree with them. It is helpful to notice what others are sensing. Even if you currently don't see or smell or taste the same thing as them, you may find that you do the next time you taste the wine.

6. Spit

This is not an obligatory part of 5S, but it is important nonetheless. People who attend wine tastings often spit their wine out instead of swallowing it. This keeps them from becoming intoxicated and gives them the option of going back for a glass of their favorite wine. Of course, when you spit the wine out, you don't get a chance to really evaluate the finish, but you can always try it again if you really like it.

If you are using a spittoon (an opaque receptacle made especially for this purpose), spit slowly against its side and not directly into the bottom. If you spit into the bottom, you might get splattered (and trust me—you don't want to get splattered). I recommend keeping a napkin handy as well.

Wine Words

I think wine descriptions are very funny. People may say a wine smells like blackberries, but what if you asked a group of people to smell a container of actual blackberries and describe the smell? What would they say? "It smells like blackberries!" Just about every descriptor in the world is used to describe a wine except for the word *grape*. For some reason, that is one word you just won't find as a descriptor on the back of a bottle or in a wine magazine.

Of course, if you smell grapes in a wine, that is fine by me. Where you are from, what you eat, and what you are familiar with affects how you describe a wine. For instance, how many people in the United States know what a lychee tastes like? Would you ever say a wine tasted or smelled like lychee? Probably not. But for people in Singapore, saying a wine has lychee flavors is perfectly normal.

Start with this comforting thought: whatever you sense is correct. Even if all you can think of is "winey," that is fine. You never know what flavors you will find. One time my wife brought me a glass of wine, and when I held it to my nose, I immediately smelled a fruit fly. Yes, fruit flies have a distinct smell, and it's not good.

"I can't drink this. I smell a fruit fly," I told her.

"That's amazing," said my wife, shaking her head. "It was only in there for two seconds! I got it out of there before I gave it to you."

So if you ever suspect that you smell something really odd in your wine (even a fruit fly), don't discount the feeling.

To start quantifying what you sense, ask yourself some questions:

a. Is it pleasant? Do you like it or dislike it?
b. Is the wine fresh, sweet, dry, oily, musty, tart, sour, bitter?
c. Is the wine tannic like espresso or fruity like apple juice?
d. If it's tannic, is it more like coffee, black tea, or green tea? Is it like tobacco? Is it delicate, like a wooden toothpick? Maybe it's like a bitter chocolate or unsweetened cocoa.
e. If it's fruity, is it like a red fruit? Maybe it is reminiscent of berries or plums. The wine may even smell like limes, pineapple, or kiwi. And yes, maybe it even tastes like grapes.

Remember that flavors should never be added to wine. Wine words are used to describe the flavors the wine acquires through the fermentation, aging, and decanting processes. If you want more ideas for wine words you can use to describe the flavors and smells you could detect, see the back of the book for a list of just some of the hundreds of common descriptors.

Different Place, Different Taste

As you already know, the amount of time the bottle has been open, the shape of the glass you are using, and the food you are eating all impact your perception of a wine. Wine is so subjective that even your mood can play a part. But did you know that the air you breathe also impacts the smell and taste of wine?

Have you ever noticed that when you get off of an airplane, the air smells different from what you are used to? Air varies thanks to climate, pollution, season, pollen counts, and multitudinous other factors. After a few seconds, you become accustomed to the local air and stop noticing it. This local air becomes the base for your olfactory senses. Naturally, the smell and taste of a wine change because of the air.

Oftentimes people tell me about a wonderful wine they had while visiting a winery in a foreign country. They loved the wine so much they bought a dozen bottles to take home. A couple of months later they opened the wine only to find that it didn't match their meticulous notes at all. This is likely because of the distinctive air in the two countries.

At PengWine, Max and I do not taste and blend our wines in the winery. Instead we do our tastings in the middle of our vineyard, where the breezes coming from the Pacific Ocean can clear our senses. Most winemakers blend and taste all their wines in their wineries, but because they're already smelling the winery, everything they put in their mouths is skewed. My wines taste different to me in each country I visit, but at least I taste them in multiple environments before selling them.

Slurping in Style

Using the 5S technique can help you fully enjoy wines, whether you have been drinking wine for decades or just had your first glass last week. As with any food or beverage, paying close attention and engaging multiple senses helps you be in the moment and notice the delicate distinctions of your wine. As you get more experienced, you may find that you have taken on a new role: that of the wine aficionado swirling, sniffing, and slurping at the party!

CHAPTER 11

Wine and Dine:
How to Order Wine in Restaurants

When I go to a restaurant with friends or family, I am often asked to choose a few bottles of wine for the table. I understand why others feel more comfortable letting me order; what would happen if someone ordered the wrong wine with a winemaker at the table? Little do they know that sometimes I look at an entire wine list and don't recognize a single brand!

If this happens to you—and it very well might—don't give up. You can still choose what to order and get through the ceremony of approving the wine unscathed. And if the wine you are served is no good, you can handle that like an expert as well.

Choosing Wine at a Restaurant

When choosing a wine for your table, think of others first. Consider who else is in the dinner party and what their budgets might be. Not everyone agrees on the ideal cost of a bottle of wine. Will the check be split at the end of the night, or is someone picking up the tab? It can't hurt to ask this before you order.

After you have some idea of the budget, ponder how many bottles you need. If there are only a few people present, you will likely drink only one bottle, and you should try to find one to suit everyone. If you are at a dinner for two, you love red wine, and your partner likes white wine, either someone has to make a sacrifice, or you can forget the bottle and order wine by the glass. If you have a large group, you should order a few bottles to suit various tastes.

Once you know your budget, as well as who prefers white and who prefers red, stop asking questions. Otherwise it will never end. There is no wine to please everyone (unless it is free, and that is not likely to happen in a restaurant).

Pairing with Food

A restaurant with a smaller wine list (ten to thirty wines) should have a selection that complements their food. Not all restaurants have put much thought into pairing, though. When this happens, it is all up to you. If your party is eating a particular cuisine, then there are likely a handful of wines that are more suitable than others. In any case, as you already know, consider the whole composition of the dishes and what you suspect may be the dominant flavors of the dishes before choosing a pairing. A pairing app can be helpful in a pinch.

Let's say you order a bottle and it complements your meal perfectly. You are having a great dinner, and the first bottle is empty before you know it. You order another bottle only to be informed that there is no more of that wine available. What do you do? Look at the wine list and try to find a wine that is similar to the original wine in both style and price. I would order a slightly more expensive wine and ask the restaurant to honor the price of the original bottle. Usually the restaurant will consent.

On the Menu

A wine menu with dozens (or even hundreds) of options, many of them in foreign languages, can be perplexing. When in doubt, use these simple tips to find the right wine for your meal and your wallet.

Sweet Deals

When I don't know which wine to order, I focus immediately on the cheapest and second-cheapest wines on the list. These wines are often the most popular, but the restaurant does not necessarily make the most profit from them. The second-cheapest wine is normally the best value on the list, even though it is sometimes ridiculed (just look up CollegeHumor's video "Second Cheapest Wine").

How are you supposed to know if the cheapest and second-cheapest wines are any good? Often they are served by the glass, which means there is probably an open bottle behind the bar. If you say you are considering ordering a bottle of the wine but that you want to try it first, most restaurants will bring you a free taste. If you like the cheaper wines on the list, that's fantastic! If not, at least you found out through a free sample and not by ordering a whole bottle.

By the Glass

If you need only one or two glasses of wine, don't consider buying a bottle unless you really like the wine and can take what is left over home with you. Instead, consider buying wines by the glass. At nice restaurants with large wine selections, the sommelier often puts good deals and pairings on this smaller list.

Typically a bottle of wine is a better value than several glasses of wine, but I find that not all restaurants do their math correctly. If five glasses of wine cost less than a bottle, by all means forgo the bottle and buy five glasses of wine.

House Wines

Restaurants frequently offer at least one white and one red wine by the glass. These are normally called the house red and white wines. The house wines are generally either the best deal the restaurant gets from the distributor or a promotional agreement made between the two businesses. These wines also sometimes come from a private label made just for the restaurant or are made by the family that owns the restaurant.

At most eateries, the cost of a bottle of house wine must be paid for within the first two glasses sold. This means that the next three pours are on the profit side, so servers can be generous about giving out samples. Remember to ask for a taste before you order!

A word of caution: because house wines are generally standard or fast wines, they don't last more than a day after being opened. Restaurants should really keep track of how long bottles have been open, but many do not. I end up returning glasses of house wine almost half of the time because the wine is oxidized. Don't be afraid to send a glass back if the wine tastes flat or exhibits other signs of oxidation.

Wine Flights

I love ordering wine flights (small samples of three to six different but complementary wines) at restaurants. Tasting numerous wines is very fun, and flights are a great way to learn how wines interact with food. If you remember to take notes, this can make you better at pairing wine with meals in the future.

A flight of wines should have a unifying factor, be it a region, a grape variety, or a wine-making style. For example, a flight may consist of a pinot noir from New Zealand, a pinot noir from the United States, and a Burgundy from France. All the wines are made from the same grapes, but that is where the similarities end.

Insider tip: If you see flights on a menu but a bottle of wine makes more sense, you should be able to sample all the wines in the flights prior to ordering an entire bottle.

Corkage Fees

As a winemaker, I often need to take wine with me to meals at fine restaurants and sometimes even to casual cafés and bistros. What if you want to take a special bottle of wine with you to a restaurant? Nearly every restaurant makes a large part of its profits from the sale of alcohol, and it's important that the restaurant does not lose money because you brought your own wine. Therefore, restaurants usually charge corkage fees to customers who bring their own wine.

Corkage fees vary greatly, so ask prior to opening your own bottle. I have been quoted a wide range of prices for bringing my own wine. Restaurants that don't have a license to sell alcohol usually have lower corkage fees than those that have alcohol licenses. Some restaurants charge a corkage fee that is equal to the price of their cheapest bottle of wine. Some have a flat rate equal to two glasses of house wine. I have even been told that the restaurant will waive the fee if I buy a bottle of wine. Regardless of the corkage fee, I often offer a taste of my wine to the sommelier. After all, wine should be shared.

In some parts of the world you are actually expected to bring your own wine to restaurants. Often, these restaurants are unable to get liquor licenses, so instead they open a wine shop next door and allow customers to bring their own wine. I've seen this done in Australia, Italy, the UK, and even in the United States. If you find a restaurant like this, you get to take your own wine free of charge.

Insider tip: If you bring your own wine, especially for the main course, immediately have your server open and decant it. This will help the wine open up by the time the meal comes.

Approving Wines

Even after you pick your wines for the evening, your job isn't over. It's time to go through the ceremony of approving the wine. What a great tradition—the ability to accept or reject the wine you selected.

There are very few restaurants that ask you to approve your food prior to serving it. I can recall this happening to me on only a few occasions. Once, a steak was brought to the table for my approval prior to cooking. Another time, the same thing happened with a whole lobster. I certainly cannot recall ever being asked if uncooked broccoli was to my satisfaction.

There are a few reasons why the entire approval process is repeated with every bottle of wine. Many years ago, prior to many technological advances in the food and beverage industry, approximately 30 percent of wines had faults. Thus, bottles of wine were always evaluated before serving. The evaluation process used to be conducted by a sommelier or wine steward, but nowadays the position is not as common. Today, the customer approves the wine by following these three steps.

Insider tip: Remember that the purpose of the wine-approval ceremony is not to decide if you like the wine you ordered! It is to confirm that the wine has no faults.

1. Reading the Label

The ceremony begins when the server presents you with the wine you ordered, showing you the front label. The server should mention the name of the wine, the variety or region where it is from, and the vintage. Make sure that the bottle matches the description in the wine list. If the wine is not the listed vintage, it is often younger than the listed bottle. I would be skeptical if the wine is older than the listed bottle. Regardless of vintage, make sure the bottle is not a lower-tier wine from the same producer. Some restaurants list a premium wine but actually stock something from the same winemaker that isn't quite as nice. If the wine is not exactly as specified on the wine list, request the correct wine or a discount before the bottle is opened.

2. Inspecting the Cork

Once you approve the bottle, the server will open it. Assuming the wine has a cork and not a screw cap, the server may ask if you mind if the wine is opened behind the bar. This happens when the server is not comfortable using a cork puller and does not wish to make a scene.

After the bottle is uncorked (at the table or otherwise), the cork will be placed in front of you for your inspection. Please do not smell the cork! It is placed before you for inspection, not sniffing. Ensure that it is not deteriorating and that the bottle did not leak. There should not be signs of wine all the way down the cork. Even if you notice a problem—even if the cork breaks into a dozen pieces—the wine could still be fine. If this happens, just be extra careful when evaluating the wine.

I find it funny when the server places a screw cap on the table. Whatever you do, do not smell the cap. You could cut your nose, and that would not be cool. If the wine has a screw cap and is over five years old, though, pay close attention (if the cap is plastic, I would be even more skeptical). Screw-cap wines can now cellar for longer as technology improves; I have had a couple of good wines with screw caps that were seven years old. But in general, screw-cap wines don't last longer than five years.

3. Checking the wine for faults

Now the server should pour a small taste of wine for you. Take your time, and remember the 5S technique. There is no rush, and you may need a couple of sips before you feel comfortable approving the wine. Start with the color; if a white wine is very golden or a red wine is brick colored or almost brown, be wary. If a wine is bad, you will most often be able to tell by the smell alone. As you might recall, the aroma should be pleasing, devoid of vinegar, wet cardboard, or nail polish remover notes. These scents are indications that the wine has disintegrated. A faulty wine may exhibit these flavors or just taste flat and lifeless.

If the wine is faulty, what should you do? If the wine is the wrong color, then you can start by pointing that out to the server. If the wine smells and tastes faulty, you have the right to ask the server to bring you another bottle. I know this can be a bit embarrassing, but these things happen. Likely the server will discuss the faulty wine with the manager, and the manager will either offer you another bottle of the same wine or recommend an alternative.

Again, the approval process is not for you to decide if you like the wine. However, if you really hate the wine, you can discuss your options with the server. If the establishment agrees to let you purchase a different bottle, don't push your luck returning a second bottle unless it has a fault.

Decanting at a Restaurant

You already know that decanting is important for many fine wines. But if a restaurant decants wine after you order it, they will probably bring it over to your table immediately and fill everyone's glass. That's hardly worth it. How can you get around this? There are a few ways:

Plan Ahead

Some restaurants allow you to call ahead and order a specific wine. They decant it for you in advance if you give them your credit card number.

Order Several Wines

Even if you do not order ahead, you could order several wines soon after you sit down. Start with an approachable wine to begin the evening, such as a sparkling wine or a young white wine. Order a more mature wine to have later with the dinner, and ask the server to decant that bottle prior to the meal.

Order Pre-Decanted Wines

I have been to restaurants that offer wines by the glass that have been decanting for five or more hours. The wine is only sold by the glass, and once all the wine from that bottle is sold, they don't open another. I wish more restaurants did this, since there are not many times you can order a glass of wine that is over fifty years old!

Good Food, Good Wine

Ordering wine at a restaurant can be a lot of fun. It is a great chance to taste new wines and enjoy good company. But if you are having dinner with ten people, you can expect to have ten completely different likes and dislikes. But by knowing where to look on the wine list, asking for samples, and properly approving wines, you can keep your entire table happy.

CONCLUSION

If you have read this whole book, you know a lot more about wine than the average person. I hope that you have gleaned some interesting facts, helpful tips, and practical knowledge that you can use as you continue to explore new wines. You should know that you have chosen a wonderful time to learn more about this fruity beverage. Wine has been bringing people together for thousands of years, and the twenty-first century promises to be one of the best yet.

As the citizens of this planet become more interconnected, wine becomes more valuable. Middle classes are growing around the world. More people are going to public places to socialize than ever before. There are more restaurants, more hotels, and more opportunities for wine to be shared. And with the support of social media, we share every moment. I'm sure that photos of wine rank pretty high in the digital world, along with photos of food, babies, cats, sunsets, and feet on beaches.

Communities are built around every product and idea out there, and the wine community is one of the fastest-growing examples. As the community expands, so does consumer awareness, curiosity, and ultimately expectation. Eventually, I hope that wine drinkers will transform the wine industry into a cleaner, healthier entity that values quality over quantity.

I am excited to find out just how fermented grape juice will evolve in this new age. In the meantime, remember that you are a part of this global wine-drinking community. Keep expanding your palate and trying new wines. Keep drinking what you like, what you can afford, and what fits your values and expectations. And, most importantly, keep raising your glass and wishing all the best to your friends and family. Cheers to you, and good luck as you continue on your wine journey.

More Wine Grape Varieties

Red Wine Grapes

cabernet franc (cab-er-nay frahnk): The godfather of the grape varieties. It gave birth to cabernet sauvignon after it was crossbred with sauvignon blanc. We at PengWine love this grape, which smells like violets.

carmenere (car-men-er): The carmenere grape variety was believed to have gone extinct until the 1990s. It was actually hiding in Chilean vineyards, where it was being mistaken as merlot. The carmenere grape takes a long time to ripen and has a very thin skin. When it rains, the grapes can literally explode on the vines in order to drop their seeds. However, the struggle is worth it: carmenere juice makes a delicious, rich wine. The spelling of this grape used to have an accent over the second e. That has since been universally removed.

zinfandel (zin-fan-dell): California is known for zinfandel, but this grape variety is originally from Italy. It makes a nice, spicy wine, and *zinfandel* is fun to say. Regrettably, white zinfandel (the cheap pink wine) has besmirched the zinfandel name. Zinfandel is a red grape, and white zinfandel is pink. I think that a lot of wine sold as white zinfandel is just leftover white wines and red wines blended together; it probably isn't from the zinfandel grape at all.

malbec (mall-beck): A very underrated grape variety from Cahors, France. Argentina has also become very famous for this variety. The skin of the malbec grape is very intense, and it adds strong tannins to the wine. It takes time for this wine to soften and develop, and even a simple malbec cellars for five years. It's great when it's at least ten years old. Unfortunately, most malbec is consumed immediately.

petit verdot (peh-teat vehr-dough): A blending grape. It's very rare to find a 100 percent petit verdot, but this variety makes a nice backbone for cabernet sauvignon and merlot.

pinotage (pea-no-taj): A great variety from South Africa that's gaining popularity around the world but still has room to grow. It took the French hundreds of years to master grape varieties in certain regions, and while technology is speeding things up, I have not found a consistent pinotage yet. I'm curious to see how it continues to develop in the next few decades.

mourvèdre (moo-veh-druh): This Spanish grape is also found in Chile, Australia, and California. It has a distinctive, pleasant smell with a long finish. First-time drinkers are always very surprised that the smell does not match the taste. Unfortunately, it is not readily available in wine stores.

Italian and Spanish reds: If you want to dive into Old World wines, your palate and pocketbook will appreciate Italian and Spanish wines. In my opinion, wines under ten dollars from Italy and Spain are a better value than equally priced wines from the United States or France.

There are so many grape varieties in these regions that there is no way I could list them all. Italy has nearly one thousand, and Southern Italy produces more wine than all of Australia. There are 350 grape varieties in Italy that are considered common (in comparison, there are just a handful of common wine grapes in the States).

Spain has over four hundred native grape varieties, but 80 percent of Spanish wines come from just twenty grape varieties. You may have heard of tempranillo, grenache, and mouvedre, the three most popular red grape varieties in Spain.[19]

White Wine Grapes

sémillon (seh-mee-own): This French grape variety is gaining popularity in Australia. Sémillon has a high acid content that allows it to cellar longer than other white wines.

muscat (muss-cat): Also known as moscato in Italy, this grape makes sweet, floral, low-alcohol wines. The muscat grape is also used to make Chilean *pisco*, a popular colorless or yellowish-to-amber brandy that does things that tequila can't do.

gewürztraminer (geh-vurts-raw-meaner): Famous for its aroma, gewürztraminer is often a little bit sweet. Many Americans just call it "gevurtz" because that's fairly easy to say.

viognier (vee-own-yay): A very sexy, voluptuous French grape variety. It's commonly blended with shiraz and other red wines because it provides a good body. If made well, viognier can cellar for a considerable amount of time.

Spanish whites: White grapes from Spain include albariño from Galicia, macabeo, palomino, and airen. There are also several popular cava (Spanish champagne) grapes, including parellada, xarel·lo, and macabeo. Cava is a great, cheaper alternative to the French stuff.

Wine-Tasting Terminology

Red Wine

Starter Descriptors

- alcoholic
- fruity
- oaky
- smoky
- earthy
- farmy
- musky

Intermediate Descriptors

- spices: cloves, cinnamon, sage, star anise, tobacco
- nuts
- jams and sauces
- fruit: fig, plum, blueberry, raspberry

The Bizarre

- cheap cigarette
- new car
- eucalyptus

White Wine

Starter Descriptors

- yeasty
- bready
- floral

- citrusy
- oaky

Intermediate Descriptors

- fruit: orange, apple, grapefruit, coconut, kiwi, lime, passion fruit, capsicum
- greens: lemongrass, asparagus, green pepper

Bad Smells (Faulty or Corked Wines)

- nail polish remover
- vinegar
- wet cardboard
- wet dog
- bad eggs

First-Time Wine Drinker's List

If you are new to wine, start with the first white wine and work your way down. The first wines on the list are sweeter, easy-drinking wines; the ones near the end of the lists are more nuanced and require a more developed palate to be fully appreciated.

If you have been drinking wines for a while, you can still benefit from this list! Start with the first wine you are not familiar with, be it a varietal or a region, then skip to the next new wine.

White Wines

1. Riesling from Alsace, France or Germany
2. Moscato from Italy
3. Pinot grigio from Italy, the United States, or Australia
4. Sauvignon blanc from France and Chile and compare them to New Zealand
5. Oaked sauvignon blanc from anywhere
6. Unoaked chardonnay
7. Oaked chardonnay

Red Wines

1. Grenache (garnacha) from Spain
2. Shiraz from Australia
3. Zinfandel from California
4. Merlot from California
5. Cabernet sauvignon from anywhere
6. Italian reds
7. Pinot noir from California, Oregon, New Zealand, or France

Food-and-Wine Pairings

Red wines	Food pairings
cabernet sauvignon	• fatty grilled, braised, charred, or roasted red meats (e.g., steak, venison, duck, pork, and lamb) • mild cheeses like cheddar, mozzarella, and brie • dark chocolate
merlot	• grilled and charred red meats (e.g., duck, beef, pork, rabbit, veal, and lamb) • seafood like tuna, salmon, and shellfish • mushroom-based vegetable dishes • mild cow- or goat-milk cheeses
pinot noir	• lightly flavored grilled, roasted, or sautéed red meats (e.g., beef, duck, ham, and quail) • seafood with distinct flavors, like salmon and tuna • earthy-flavored sauces made with mushrooms, truffles, and vegetables
sangiovese	• Italian dishes like pasta, meatballs, spaghetti, and pizza with a tomato base • bland meat dishes like meatloaf and roast chicken
shiraz	• heavily seasoned and flavorful red meat dishes (e.g., beef stew, steak, venison, lamb, pork chops, roast duck, and brisket)
cabernet franc	• classic French bistro foods • roast chicken • red meat dishes
carmenére	• rich meat dishes like stews, lamb, steak, and barbecue

zinfandel	• spicy dishes like beef or pork in pepper sauce • sauces with tomato bases and herbs (like oregano and basil)
malbec	• rich meat dishes like stews, lamb, steak, and barbecue • earthy-flavored sauces that contain herbs, mushrooms, and truffles
petit verdot	• rich cuts of red meat • wild game • aged cheeses
pinotage	• grilled, braised, or smoked red meats like beef and wild game • earthy-flavored sauces and vegetables like herbs, mushrooms, and truffles
mourvèdre	• grilled, braised, or smoked red meats like beef and wild game • earthy-flavored sauces that contain herbs, mushrooms, and truffles

White wines	Food pairings
chardonnay	• flavorful and fatty seafood dishes like tuna, salmon, shrimp, and sea bass • white meats like chicken, pork, and turkey • rich sauces made with herbs, cream, and butter
riesling	• simple chicken, seafood, or meat dishes like oysters, veal, and lean shellfish • sweet and spicy dishes • desserts such as apple pie
pinot grigio	• light seafood dishes like oysters • light meat dishes like ham, chicken, and veal • pasta and ravioli
sauvignon blanc	• seafood dishes like crab, oysters, shrimp, scallops, and other crustaceans • white meats like chicken, pork, and turkey • tangy or slightly acidic sauces and dressings

sémillon	• simple light dishes made with chicken, shellfish, or fish
muscat	• sweet desserts that contain fresh fruit • cheese and antipasto platters
gewürztraminer	• white meats like chicken, fish, and turkey • fresh fruit and sweet desserts that contain fruits
viognier	• fish like bluefish and mackerel • spicy dishes like Indian, Thai, and Ethiopian cuisine

1 "Cities of Iran," *Iran Chamber Society*, accessed August 15, 2015, http://www.iranchamber.com/cities/shiraz/shiraz.php.

2 Stephanie Pappas, "Facts About Sulfur," *Live Science*, November 24, 2014, http://www.livescience.com/28939-sulfur.html.

3 "Bordeaux Grands Crus Classés en 1855," *Bordeaux*, accessed August 5, 2015, http://www.bordeaux.com/us/vineyard/bordeaux-wine-classifications.

4 "Complete Guide to First Growth Bordeaux Wine and Chateau," *Wine Cellar Insider*, accessed August 15, 2015, http://www.thewinecellarinsider.com/wine-topics/bordeaux-growth-wine-guide/.

5 "Resveratrol Supplements," *WebMD*, accessed August 11, 2015, http://www.webmd.com/heart-disease/resveratrol-supplements.

6 "Phylloxera," *Phylloxera and Grape Industry Board of South Australia*, accessed August 15, 2015, http://www.phylloxera.com.au/bio-security/phylloxera/.

7 Jordan Ross, "Yield versus Quality," *Enology International*, accessed August 15, 2015, http://www.enologyinternational.com/yield/yieldvsq7.html.

8 Ray Isle, "The Battle for America's Oldest Vines," *Food & Wine*, October 2013, http://www.foodandwine.com/articles/the-battle-for-americas-oldest-vines.

9 Glenn McGourty, "Cover Cropping Systems for Organically Farmed Vineyards," *Practical Winery & Vineyard Journal*, September/October 2004, http://www.practicalwinery.com/septoct04/septoct04p22.htm.

10 Carrie Schulte, "Wine Barrels: How They Effect the Flavor and Price of Our Wines," *Constant Contact,* accessed August 15, 2015, http://library.constantcontact.com/download/get/file/1110153099501-52/About+Wine+Barrels.pdf.

11 "The Cooperage Markets of Chile and the Island of Trinidad," *National Coopers Journal* 32, no. 1 (1916): 26, Google Books, https://books.google.com/books?id=2_FYAAAAYAAJ&lpg=RA1-PA26&ots=tTlHrGGXGw&dq=rauli%20wood%20wine%20barrels%20chile&pg=RA1-PA26#v=onepage&q=rauli%20wood%20wine%20barrels%20chile&f=false.

12 "Top 100 Cellar Selections 2011: The Year's Most Important Collectibles," *Wine Enthusiast Magazine*, December 1, 2011, http://www.winemag.com/PDFs/122011_CellarSelections.pdf.

13 "Beaujolais Nouveau Day," *Party Excuses*, accessed August 14, 2015, http://www.beaujolaisnouveauday.com/.

14 Emanuella Grinberg, "Should You Be Worried about Arsenic in California Wine?," *CNN*, March 29, 2015, http://www.cnn.com/2015/03/27/living/arsenic-wine-california-lawsuit-feat/.

15 H. Vally and P. Thompson, "Role of Sulfite Additives in Wine Induced Asthma: Single Dose and Cumulative Dose Studies," *Thorax* 56, no. 10 (2001): 763–69, http://www.ncbi.nlm.nih.gov/pmc/articles/PMC1745927/.

16 *The Costco Craze: Inside the Warehouse Giant*, CNBC, April 26, 2012, http://www.cnbc.com/id/46603589.

17 P. Govinda, "Oxidized Wines," *Imbibe*, August 14, 2009, http://imbibemagazine. com/oxidized-wines/.

18 "Michel Rolland," *Wikipedia*, last modified March 12, 2016, http://en.wikipedia. org/wiki/Michel_Rolland.

19 "Spanish Wine," *Wikipedia*, last modified January 19, 2016, https://en.wikipedia. org/wiki/Spanish_wine.

There are many people that have been a part of my wine journey. In recognition to all of you

Kate Goodman
Craig Thornbury
Max Eyzaguirre
Adam Marks
Richard Fleischman
Mike Borchert
Brian Bozan
Marc Collins
Heather light Grieves
Marni Rogow
Eric Rogow
Ish Moreno
Tim Geiser
Joel Trueblood
Eugenio Amenabar
Kevin Cox
Eric Cohen
My KPI group
Eric Silverman
Marc Tragler
Duncan Dieter
Christopher Moore
Shawn Lee
Jamie Chatterton
Robert Stanbary
Cassandra Allen
Christian Eyzaguirre

Horacio Eyzaguirre
Dell Taylor
Louis-Antione Luyt
Pablo Varas
Piotr Poznanski
Kanthi Junkeer
Eve Lai
Jody Pearch
Roderic Proniewski
Sally Ong
Flora Loh
Max Morales
Hector Olivares
Tito Morande
Ed Flaherty
Olivia Sari
Danielle Thompson
David LeClaire
Toni Dudzak
Karen Gelfond
Fran Walker
Bill Milliken
Goldie Milliken
Jim Milliken
Mike Denny
Nigel Simonsz
Zainal Abdul Kadir

INDEX

A

additional ingredients, 30–31
aerators, 62
aging stage, 17, 20–22, 71
Ah-So two-prong cork puller, 63
airen (grape variety), 95
albariño (grape variety), 95
alcohol burn, 41–42
Alvarez-Peters, Annette, 48
apple wine, 12
approval process, of wine ordered in
        restaurants, 86–87
apps
        for finding wines you like, 44
        for keeping labels purchased, 67
Argentinian wine, 49–50
aroma-training kits, 65
arsenic, 31
awards
        influence of on pricing, 50
        as publicized on bottle, 33

B

Bacchus, 5
bag-in-box packaging, 36–37
barrel fermentation, 19, 20
Beaujolai nouveau, 26, 27
biodynamic wines, 32–33, 37
blends, 22
Bordeaux region (France), 5–6, 22
Bordeaux Wine Classification of
        1855, 5
botrytis wine, 12
boxes (as packaging), 36

breathing (of wine), 70
buying direct, 52

C

cabernet franc (grape variety), 6, 10, 22,
        93, 99
cabernet sauvignon (grape variety), xiv,
        xvi, 6, 10, 12, 22, 42, 56, 93, 94,
        98, 99
Californian wine, 49
canister, 66
cans (as packaging), 36
carmenere (grape variety), 28, 93, 99
cartons (as packaging), 36
cava (grape variety), 95
cellaring, 11, 13, 25, 31, 68, 69, 73,
        87, 93
Champagne province, 13, 25
chardonnay (grape variety), xv, 11, 56,
        57, 68, 98, 100
Charles Shaw, 31
Château Haut-Brion, 6
Château Lafite Rothschild, 6
Château Latour, 6
Château Margaux, 6
Château Mouton Rothschild, 6
cherry wine, 12
Chile, as only wine-producing country
        with no phylloxera, 13
Chilean wine, xvi, 6, 13, 20, 23, 27, 49
Christianity, role of in spread of wine, 5
coasters, 66
cork, breakage of, 70
cork pullers, 35, 69, 70
cork stoppers, 33–35, 36

cork taint, 34–35, 77
corkage fees, 85–86
Costco, 47–48
counterfeit wines, 53

D

decanters, 62
decanting, 71, 72–73, 87–88
Dionysus, 5
distributors, 47
double-lever corkscrew, 63, 66
Douro region (Portugal), 13
drip controllers, 64
DropStop, pour discs, 64, 66

E

electric wine openers, 63, 66

F

fast wines, 24, 25–26, 27, 85
fermentation stage, 17, 19–20
First Growth Bordeaux wineries, 6
first press, 18, 19
first use (oak barrel), 20
5S technique (for wine tasting), 75–79,
    81, 87
flipflop, 31
France
    belief that best wines come from, 5
    production regulations in, 32
Franzia, 31
free-flow juices, 18, 19
French standard, 32, 37
fruit wines, 12
fume blanc (white wine), 12

G

gamay (grape variety), 26
gewürztraminer (grape variety), 95, 101
glasses, 61–62, 65–66

grape varieties
    airen, 95
    albariño, 95
    cabernet franc, 6, 10, 22, 93, 99
    cabernet sauvignon, xiv, xvi, 6,
        10, 12, 22, 42, 56, 93, 94,
        98, 99
    carmenere, 28, 93, 99
    cava, 95
    chardonnay, xv, 11, 56, 57, 68,
        98, 100
    gamay, 26
    gewürztraminer, 95, 101
    grenache, 84, 98
    macabeo, 95
    malbec, 22, 93–94, 100
    merlot, xiv, 6, 10, 12, 22, 28, 33,
        68, 93, 94, 98, 99
    moscato, 95, 98
    mourvèdre, 94, 100
    muscat, 9, 95, 101
    palomino, 95
    parellada, 95
    petit verdot, 6, 22, 94, 100
    pinot grigio, xiv, 11, 25, 28,
        98, 100
    pinot meunier, 9
    pinot noir, 9, 10, 11, 85, 98, 99
    pinotage, 94, 100
    riesling, 11, 12, 25, 56, 98, 100
    sangiovese, 10, 99
    sauvignon blanc, xv, 10, 11, 12, 25,
        77, 93, 98, 100
    sémillon, 11, 95, 101
    shiraz, 4, 10–11, 95, 98, 99
    syrah, 4
    tempranillo, 94
    Vidal, 12
    viognier, 95, 101
    xarel·lo, 95
    zinfandel, 93, 98, 100

Great Britain, as one of first and best customers of French wine, 6
green bottles, reason for, 69
grenache (grape variety), 84, 98

H

harvest, description of, 17–18
hosted events
    buying wine for, 57
    receiving wine at, 58
hot spiced wines, 74
house wines, 84–85

I

ice bucket, 66
ice wine, 12
importers, 47
insulator, 66
Italian red grapes, 94, 98

K

kiwi wine, 12

L

label removers, 66, 67
labels, 30–33
Le Creuset, table wine opener, 63, 66
lever corkscrew, 63
lychee wine, 12

M

macabeo (grape variety), 95
malbec (grape variety), 22, 93–94, 100
mango wine, 12
Mediterranean cuisine, as easiest to pair with wines, 57
merlot (grape variety), xiv, 6, 10, 12, 22, 28, 33, 68, 93, 94, 98, 99
micro-oxygenation, 71–72

Mondovino (documentary), 71
moscato (grape variety), 95, 98
mourvèdre (grape variety), 94, 100
muscat (grape variety), 9, 95, 101
must (pulp), 16

N

Napoleon III, 5, 6
Nebuchadnezzar bottle, 36
new oak, 20
New World wines, 26, 27, 28, 30
1990 Stags Leap, xiii
1995 Viu Manent Reserva cabernet sauvignon, xvi
1997 Miguel Torres sauvignon blanc, xv
Noble One (botrytis wine), 12
nonvintage wines, 23
nose-training kits, 65
notebook, for keeping labels purchased, 66, 67

O

oak barrels
    costs of using, 37
    forging/toasting of, 21
    production of, 21
    use of in aging, 20
    use of in fermentation, 19
oak staves, use of with stainless steel tanks, 22
Old World wines, 26, 27, 28, 30
online
    wine clubs, 52
    for wine sales, 51–52
openers, 63, 66
opening (of wine), 69–70
organic wines, 32, 33, 37
oxidation, 70, 72, 85
oxygen, as friend and enemy of wine, 70–71

P

packaging, 36–37
palate, development of, 42–44
palomino (grape variety), 95
parellada (grape variety), 95
peach wine, 12
PengWine
    as author's business, xvi
    blend of chardonnay and sauvignon
        blanc, 11
    cabernet franc as a favorite grape
        of, 93
    cost of barrels purchased by, 21
    decanting of wines from, 72
    effect of 2010 earthquake on, 23
    first sales of wine from, 48–49
    outdoor blend tasting session,
        16, 81
    PengWine Emperor, 23, 54
    PengWine Rockhopper, 55
    as putting blends on labels, 22
    use of barrels at, 21
    as using stainless steel tanks, 19
Pérignon, Dom Pierre, 5, 34
petit verdot (grape variety), 6, 22,
    94, 100
phylloxera, 13, 26
piccolo bottle, 36
pinot grigio (grape variety), xiv, 11, 25,
    28, 98, 100
pinot meunier (grape variety), 9
pinot noir (grape variety), 9, 10, 11, 85,
    98, 99
pinotage (grape variety), 94, 100
port wine, 12–13
pour discs, 64, 66
pressing stage, 17, 18
Prohibition era, 5

Q

questions, to ask yourself to start
    quantifying what you sense, 80

R

rauli tree, use of in barrel making, 20
red wine
    as aging better than white wine, 9
    as commonly blended, 9, 22
    as fermented differently than white
        wine, 9
    first-time wine drinker's list, 98
    food pairings with, 99–100
    health virtues of, 9
    making of, 16, 17
    as oaked more often than white
        wine, 9
    wine-tasting terminology, 96
red wine grapes
    list of, 93–94
    most popular varieties, 10–11
    in pinot noir and pinot meunier, 9
restaurant experiences
    decanting of wine at, 87–88
    ordering of wine at, 82–87
resveratrol, 9
retailers, 47, 51
riesling (grape variety), 11, 12, 25, 56,
    98, 100
Rolland, Michael, 71, 72

S

sangiovese (grape variety), 10, 99
sauvignon blanc (grape variety), xv, 10,
    11, 12, 25, 77, 93, 98, 100
savor (as step 5 in 5S technique), 78–79
screw cap stoppers, 33, 34, 35, 36
second and third press, 18, 19
second use (oak barrel), 20

see (as step 1 in 5S technique), 76

sémillon (grape variety), 11, 95, 101

serving temperature, 73–74

shiraz (grape variety), 4, 10–11, 95, 98, 99

sip (as step 4 in 5S technique), 78

slow wines, 24–25

smartphone, for keeping track of labels purchased, 66

smell (as step 3 in 5S technique), 77–78

Spanish red grapes, 94

Spanish white grapes, 95

spit (as optional step 6 in 5S technique), 79

stainless steel, use of in fermentation, 19, 20

standard wines, 24, 25, 85

stoppers, 33–36, 64

storage (of wine), 68–69

subdistributors, 47

sulfites, 31

sulfur, role of in wine making, 4

sulfur dioxide (SO2), 31

swirl (as step 2 in 5S technique), 76–77

synthetic cork stoppers, 33, 34, 35

syrah (grape variety), 4

T

table grapes, compared to wine grapes, 8

tempranillo (grape variety), 94

terroir, 5, 6–7, 11, 13, 16, 27, 49, 77

Tokaji (Tokay) wine, 12

trichloroanisole (TCA), 34

tropical cuisines, as trickier to pair with wines, 57

V

Vidal (grape variety), 12

vinegar, health benefits of, 4

vines, age of, 13–14

vintage, 23–24, 25, 50

viognier (grape variety), 95, 101

Vivino (app), 44

W

waiter's-friend corkscrew, 63

white wine

as fermented differently than red wine, 9

first-time wine drinker's list, 98

food pairings with, 100–101

making of, 16

as not necessarily blended, 11

wine, 96–97

white wine grapes

list of, 95

most popular varieties, 11–12

wine

bringing your own to restaurants, 86

buying of for hosted event, 57

buying of wisely, 53

erroneous perceptions about, ix

evaluation of, 75–81

finding ones you like, 45

history of, 3–7

modern wine era as originating with Greeks and Romans, 4–5

nearly all as made from grape juice, 8

ordering of in restaurants, 82–87

origins of in Mesopotamia, 4

receiving of at hosted event, 58

as tasting different depending on location, 80–81

where to buy, 50–53

wine appreciation, author's journey, xi–xvi

Wine Away, 66, 67

wine cellar, 31, 68, 69

wine clubs (onlinc), 52
wine dispensers, 64–65
wine distribution, 29–30, 47
Wine Enthusiast Magazine, 25
wine fairs, 44
wine flights, 85
wine fridges, 65, 66
wine grapes, compared to table grapes, 8
wine industry
    revolution as long overdue in,
        37–38
    as unregulated, 30
wine investments, 53
wine journal, 42
wine making
    additional ingredients, 30–31
    profits in, 29
    variables in, 15
wine pairing
    cautions with conventional wisdom
        about, 54–55
    complexity of, xiii
    examples of, xiv, 99–100
    learning about, 55–57
    in restaurants, 83
wine pourers, 64

wine pricing, 49–50
wine survival kit
    decanters and aerators, 62
    openers, 63, 66
    stoppers, 33–36, 64
    wine pourers and drip
        controllers, 64
    wineglasses, 61–62, 65–66
wine words, 79–80
Wine.com, 52
wineglasses, 61–62, 65–66
winemakers, 47
wineries, for finding wines you like, 45
Wine-Searcher.com, 52
wine-tasting terminology, 96

X

xarel·lo (grape variety), 95

Y

yeast, as fueling fermentation, 19

Z

zinfandel (grape variety), 93, 98, 100